P9-DJV-054

LOCAL BOY MAKES GOOD

THREE MUSICALS BY JOHN GRAY

Talonbooks   •   Vancouver   •   1987

copyright © 1987 John Gray

published with assistance from the Canada Council

Talonbooks
201 / 1019 East Cordova Street
Vancouver
British Columbia V6A 1M8
Canada

Typeset in Garth Graphic by Pièce de Résistance Ltée.;
printed and bound in Canada by Hignell Printing Ltd.

First printing: October 1987

Rights to produce *18 Wheels, Rock and Roll,* and *Don Messer's Jubilee,* in whole or in part, in any medium by any group, amateur or professional, are retained by the author. Interested parties are requested to apply to John Gray Management Inc., 3392 W. 37th Ave., Vancouver, B.C., V6N 2V6 Canada.

Canadian Cataloguing in Publication Data

Gray, John, 1946-
  Local boy makes good

  Contents: 18 wheels - Rock and roll - Don
Messer's jubilee.
  ISBN 0-88922-248-7

  I. Title.
PS8563.R39L62 1987   C812'.54   C87-091454-5
PR9199.3.G73L62 1987

for E.P. and The Wolf

Contents

Introduction

I was brought up in Truro, Nova Scotia, a conservative distribution centre of about 12,000 inhabitants of primarily Scottish descent, with a reputation for church, education and the arts. We had an agricultural college and a teacher's college. There was a music festival and, intermittently, an amateur dramatic society, the Colchester Players, under the direction of a sign painter named Alden Irving and a hairdresser named Shirly Hamilton. The Nova Scotia Provincial Exhibition, which was on the surface an agricultural fair but was really an orgy of romance and intrigue, took place in Bible Hill every September. The Truro Bearcats hockey team played every winter, and the Truro Bearcats baseball team played every summer as a farm team for the Chicago Cubs.

As far as I was concerned, Truro was the universal norm, common knowledge to every human being on earth. What made other nations, races, and cultures more interesting than mine (and they were *all* more interesting than mine) were achievements they had acquired over and above the basic Truro upbringing, a little like the optional equipment, the chrome and the fender skirts perhaps, on an American car. My environment was not really any different from anyone else's, only cheaper, more basic; the stripped-down Chevrolet Biscayne sedan, not the Impala hardtop.

My piano teacher was a Latvian composer named Berino who

had spent the War in a Nazi prison camp and the post-War in a Stalinist prison camp. World events had lost their lustre for Mr. Berino, but not for me. For me the world was a distant flame from the South: bright, dancing, and utterly fascinating.

The flame glowed somewhere over the horizon, radiating a vague, unsatisfying warmth. It glowed brightest when I went to the movies, watched television or listened to the Hit Parade, but then it would fade and there would be Truro, more drab then ever. How could the Truro Music Festival compare to Elvis Presley? How could the Colchester Players measure up to a Warner Brothers movie?

Like an insect, I gravitated to the brighter flame.

I played in a series of rock bands named after fast American cars. Every Friday and Saturday night we played all the hits from Motown, basking in borrowed charisma. The music kept me in contact with the flame, and for my friends it put me closer to the flame than they were: obviously someone who *plays* music by Elvis Presley is closer to Elvis Presley than someone who only *listens* to music by Elvis Presley. The flame danced in the music, and in the eyes of the people who watched me play it.

Meanwhile at school we learned the basics: sheer heaven for the neoconservative educator. I studied history, science, math, English literature and grammar, French and Latin. There was one physical education class per week. Music was taught in Grade Seven (I failed), and Industrial Arts in Grades Eight and Nine, where I constructed useful scissors-holders and match-scratchers. Once in a while we were split into sexes and taught about the dangers of personal abuse.

Canadian history was taught in Grade Seven. There we learned of the victory of General James Wolfe over le Marquis de Montcalm, of the heroism of General Brock at Queenston Heights, of the treachery of the savages and their cruelty to the gentle Catholic priests, of the BNA Act, Sir John A., and the CPR.

The shortness of the curriculum gave us a general impression of a smooth drift toward Confederation thanks to Imperial visionaries like Lord Durham, in the face of truculent natives, comically incompetent farmers under Mackenzie and a bunch of poor losers under Papineau. Riel was simply out of his mind, and had to be put to sleep like a dog with distemper. Canada hiked through the twentieth century, the Good Little Buddy, the Honest Broker, blending harmoniously with all the other countries shaded in pink on the big world map with the Neilson's Chocolate advertisement in the corner. We were never confused by an excess of fact.

English Literature tended to feature short, morally instructive pieces that illustrated literary devices: description, narrative and the like. There was also some of what passed for poetry. Everyone had to memorize W. H. Davies for some reason:

> What is this life if, full of care,
> We have no time to stand and stare.
> No time to stand beneath the boughs
> And stare as long as sheep or cows.

We took this bovine advice to heart, and like sheep or cows we stared at it all indiscriminately.

I didn't know at this time that there was such a thing as a Canadian writer. In fact, upon my graduation I couldn't name with assurance a single Canadian author, poet, composer, musician or artist. I had never played a Canadian song. If there was one lesson to be learned in Truro, if there was one area where my teachers and Elvis Presley were in complete agreement, it was the knowledge that culture is something that comes from someplace else. Canada plays no music, writes no poetry, paints no pictures, makes no history. Other countries do these things for us. In these areas Canada is the one place in the world where nothing happens, a lifeless place full of dull people, can't wait to get out.

By the time I went to University it didn't matter that there were books by Canadians available to me. I didn't read them. I knew they would be dull. By then I had fully objectified the word "Canadian" as another topic for one of the many racial stereotypes I had absorbed in my youth: Natives are lazy, Blacks are stupid, Arabs are treacherous, and the Chinese put cat meat in your chop suey. And, of course, Canadians are dull. But unlike its counterparts, the Canadian stereotype is impossible to refute, implying as it does a lack of characteristics, an absence, a kind of brain damage. The Canadian stereotype is something you can't overcome, only escape. You escape nothingness by finding something, that is, by becoming somebody else.

From that point on, I set about distancing myself from Canada in spirit. I became one of those people who are stuck here by circumstance, but who really belong someplace else, someplace more sensitive, more sophisticated, more international, yes, that's it, international, part of a world of the imagination, vastly more meaningful than wherever it is we happen to be, a world free of the messiness of the here and now, free of the pettiness of real people.

And I reached the age of thirty without having written or composed a thing. What was there for me to write about that would not be Canadian, that would not be dull?

I directed British and American plays for a few years, but it became obvious that I would never be able to do British and American plays as well as the British and the Americans do, just as Canadian actors will never do British accents as well as the British can. The British simply have too much of a head start at being British.

Eventually I drifted to Toronto. I called the actor Eric Peterson and learned he was working with a company called Theatre Passe Muraille, that he was doing a history play by Rick Salutin called *1837: The Farmers' Revolt*. I didn't want to see it. I knew it would be dull.

But I was sleeping on Eric's couch, so out of politeness more than anything I drove to Listowel, Ontario, and found the sales barn where the show was playing. (A sales barn is a public barn where livestock is bought and sold at auction.) I watched a play about the revolt of southwest Ontario farmers, teachers and blacksmiths against the Family Compact, not a hundred yards from the road where Van Egmond, veteran of Trafalgar, with one leg and one arm, joined the farmers in their fight for land, power and human rights. In the final scene, Lount and Matthews, a teacher and a blacksmith, are about to be hanged for treason:

MATTHEWS: Sam. Sam, we lost.
LOUNT: No, Peter. We just haven't won, yet.

Suddenly the bean farmers and dairy farmers from Listowel in their nylon jackets and John Deere caps were on their feet with a roar that could be heard in Wingham. I was astounded. These were Canadians. Yet there they were with tears on their faces, cheering some of their ancestors who had gone down fighting.

The next day I took the streetcar to the Toronto Necropolis and searched among the gravestones until I found them. Samuel Lount and Peter Matthews, died 1837, hanged. Just across the cemetery was the grave of Mackenzie, with a wreath of fresh flowers on it.

I suppose there are cultures in the world where they take for granted the ability to see something in a book or play and then to see it in life. I suppose there are cultures where they don't assume alienness as part of the nature of art itself. And it would be difficult for them to understand what it is like to touch something you read about or saw in a play, for the first time, in your own country. All I can tell them is that it transforms the object in question, and it transforms your life as well.

I joined Theatre Passe Muraille and worked as a composer and musician under director Paul Thompson. For the first time, I found I could write songs. It's quite natural to leap into the air when your feet are on the ground.

I worked on *The Horseburgh Scandal* and *Shakespeare For Fun and Profit*, neither of which was particularly successful. But in the process of producing and performing these plays I learned a great deal about Canadian audiences, Canadian forms, and about myself and what enables me to create.

I was playing electric piano with *The Horseburgh Scandal* in Blyth, Ontario the first time I noticed that there were older audience members sitting in the spill of the stage light who weren't actually watching the performance, but who sat there with eyes cast downward, some even with hands shielding their eyes. It was a bit bizarre. They were listening carefully, and would steal quick, furtive glances at the stage whenever someting critical was going on, but it was as though the act of watching, or of being seen to watch, performers on a stage behaving as though they were alone, had a faintly obscene, voyeuristic quality that embarrassed them in some visceral way they couldn't overcome.

I remembered attending a play in Belgrade with a Yugoslavian director, and during the half-hour intervals he held my hand the entire time. Even though I knew perfectly well that this was an accepted custom with no sexual connotation at all, I couldn't overcome that vague physical queasiness that I was doing something that just *isn't done*. You don't hold hands with other gentlemen in public, not for a *half an hour* at a time. And I wonder how many of us would be able to watch an authentic Elizabethan performance of *Romeo and Juliet* cast entirely with men, and appreciate the production in quite the same way?

In Blyth, Ontario it dawned on me that for many Canadians the primary convention of nineteenth-century European theatre, the illusionistic, fourth-wall convention, was a foreign phenomenon, and why shouldn't it be? Under what circumstances does a group of people in a Canadian village watch another group of people in the same room behave as though the watchers weren't present?

Canada has no music hall tradition to draw from, no masques, no vaudeville, no puppet shows, no mysteries, no mimes. Draw from these traditions in Canada and even if people are impressed and intimidated by what they see as a superior sensibility at work, they aren't going to have a very good time. And, as Dr. Johnson said, we are here to delight and to instruct, in that order.

Just as the most avid hockey fan is the person who played hockey as a child, audience members like to have a solid sense of what is being attempted, what the whole exercise is based upon, and they like to have some first-hand knowledge of the techniques involved so that they will not be taken for suckers. If Canadians are going to regard theatre as something other than a cultural zoo, it needs to evolve from the theatre people practise in their kitchens, on the streets and in the bars, as a matter of course in their everyday lives.

The theatre Canadians practise as naturally as breathing is the theatre of the storyteller, the spellbinder in the beer parlour who silences the room when he begins a tale. Every town has its storytellers, people who can make an incident come alive over and over again, who can say something "just the way so-and-so would say it," who can make you laugh, cry, or gasp in disbelief and horror.

I suppose it goes back to the necessary skills of a small population in an immense land mass where communication is as precious as water in Saudi Arabia. But that is academic. The salient fact for me at the time was that, whenever an actor played directly to the audience in the manner of a storyteller, or sang in the manner of a beer parlour act, the audience members caught in the spill of the stage light suddenly relaxed, watched the stage closely, slapped their knees and laughed.

For me as a potential writer of musicals, that one insight was the major break of my career, for it offered a way out of the traditional American musical comedy genre that I have always despised for many reasons. I have always found American musical comedies shrill, facile and patronizing: overblown bubbles that burst the moment they touch the earth, leaving you with nothing. I am always particularly offended by the transition from illusionistic scene to presentational musical number, where you've just been manipulated into believing in the reality of an event when suddenly they turn on you for the kill. Everything turns to papier maché and everyone sings at your face, dancers flailing away with tense muscles and fixed smiles brimming with an artificial, unmotivated joie de vivre that has nothing to do with the situation at hand, but everything to do with the snake oil huckster, the con artist, the high-pressure salesperson: "Like me, like me, make me rich, make me famous, I'll kill everyone who tries to stop me..."

On the other hand, the storyteller can sing as a natural extension of the narrative. A song can be evocative, ironic, farcical or didactic: whatever is necessary to serve the story, rather than the other way around. And the storytelling situation is essentially content-oriented: it's the story itself that counts.

If I ever thought of anything to say, I had a Canadian form in which to say it. But this was Ontario, historic, culturally-enlightened Ontario, whereas I was from Truro. Characteristically, my way of becoming a Canadian in my mind was to masquerade as someone from Ontario (my mother is from Ontario, you know). The stripped-down Chevy Biscayne does not become more glamorous to the owner just because it is in a better parking lot.

On the other hand, my uncertainty about content meant that I concentrated on form and that was a good thing, for the world is replete with theatre people who think they have attained certain insights that free them from the need to develop technical skills.

The form I tackled first was songwriting, which should not be surprising since the Seventies was the decade of the singer-song-writer. Everyone who could strum three chords (sometimes two) on a guitar was trying to write Gordon Lightfoot ballads, just as in the Eighties everyone with a word processor seems to be working on a screenplay. My interests were and are unexceptional and there I was, toiling away with guitar, piano and rhyming dictionary, developing a facility with metre and rhyme that I might later apply in the theatre.

It is heresy for a North American to say this, but I am not a person who thrives on a great deal of personal freedom. When I write a song it must be for a specific situation. I have no repertoire of I-Love-You and Sorry-Baby-I-Gotta-Ramble songs, and when I write a musical I want to know what stage it is to open on, what the approximate budget will be, and who is likely to be in the audience. I like to cast the show in my imagination with familiar actors, even if those actors are no longer living. I am no modernist. The empty canvas terrifies me, and my first instinct is to construct a grid. If I am to write anything that might loosely be termed of poetic value, my best bet is to turn to a form that places strict *a priori* demands upon the writer, and no form is as confining as the popular song, with its exact rhythms, its limited number of acceptable rhyme schemes, its narrow grid. But paradoxically, it sets me free. It is the only thing I have in common with Tibetan iconographical painters.

Sigmund Freud constructed an *Architectural Digest* vision of the mind which consists of an Outer Room which receives all visitors, and an Inner Room containing a massive Eye (or, perhaps, "I"), which admits only some of these visitors. Between these two rooms is a door, and beside the door a Guard who, armed with one's preconceptions, fears and prejudices, decides which visitors may be seen by the Eye and which may not. It's a bit like an exclusive New York night club, the human consciousness, and the trick for the creative artist is to distract the Guard, admitting some unfamiliar visitors who might otherwise be banned. To do this the artist busies the Guard with seemingly arbitrary formal problems like sonnet and sonata construction. While the Guard is puzzled, new insights sneak by.

Like anyone from Truro, my Guard is beefy and well-armed. Fortunately he is easily charmed by music, speech and rhyme, and I get some work done.

The three musicals in this collection belong together for many reasons. They were all written for Canadian audiences in the spill of the stage light with their hands covering their eyes. All three have prominent narrator-storytellers and extended monologues. In all three, the songs are intended to serve the story and not the other way around. All three refer to performance situations that have nothing to do with the legitimate theatre—beer parlours, Legion Hall dances, hockey arenas, radio and television studios—yet are at the same time public places. There are no kitchens or bedrooms. The audience is not peering unnoticed through anybody's window.

The three musicals are saturated wtih a sense of place and geography; the characters tend to be defined by geographical circumstances, actual and figurative, not by class, race or ideology. This is a typically Canadian preoccupation, and it goes deeper than simple East-versus-West or Quebec-versus-Ontario regionalism: more than one youth from Truro has gone home with missing teeth from having "walked around New Glasgow as through they owned the place," and a lad from Saskatoon, Saskatchewan will find it highly significant that a girl is from Prince Albert.

The perceived "Canadian-ness" in my writing does not arise, as some people think, out of any deeply-felt political nationalism on my part, but out of the common human desire to know who and where I am, to do things that could not have been done by somebody else, to cause something consciously, to be something other than a walking, talking symptom. I didn't choose to be formed in Canada but there it is, and I am still looking for information. I enjoy wracking my brains trying to figure out how the puzzle fits together, even though I know there will be a piece missing in the end.

What these musicals most obviously have in common is their subject matter. They are all about bands; not the rich, famous bands from someplace else that dominate the airwaves, but the local bands, cultural weeds that grow whether we think we want them or not. I have often thought that the fragility we ascribe to Canadian culture is the natural result of alienated, self-conscious, contrived, hothouse cultivation. We spend too much time trying to produce blooms that will appeal to what we see as a superior, more civilized sensibility, and not enough time on the local flora and fauna. So we are left with a fragile bouquet that wilts in the natural environment.

Every town and village in Canada has had a local band at one time or another along with a local storyteller, and it would not occur to their audience to suggest that what they do is art. It is too indigenous, too familiar, too comprehensible to be called art. To enjoy the local band you don't have to know anything you do not already know. The local band is playing for your and their pleasure, not for some other, unknown reason.

But for me the local band *is* art, far more than the travelling dance companies performing excerpts from *Swan Lake* and imitation Twyla Tharp, the touring productions of *Private Lives* and the community concert string quartets, all the more so because the local band is not *trying* to be art, an enterprise that in Canada usually means imitating something from someplace else.

I am sometimes troubled by the uneasy sensation that I imitate my subject matter, consciously cultivating work that has the indigenous qualities of the local weeds, the unlabelled art that is rarely recognized here and now but is around us all the same, mocking our ongoing attempt to grasp our lives. Maybe I am like the characters in *Rock and Roll*: by acknowledging through imitation what was unacknowledgeable in the past I am able to keep faith that the present will one day make sense.

It's an uneasy contortion, but at least it produces plays that do not look like other plays. My audience can enter the theatre, look at the stage, and feel the pleasurable anticipation that, whatever they are about to experience, it will come in a form that has given them pleasure in the past: anything to avoid that faint, depressing premonition that one is about to undergo "art."

A reading of these musicals leaves out one essential element, the music, and I'm glad. The lyrics take days to write, while the tunes just bubble up out of the unconscious as though they've always been there, and it's vaguely disheartening to know that the tunes are what audiences remember while the lyrics are barely heard, with only the repeated "hook" sticking in the memory. Unlike recordings, musicals are written to be heard once, and I have often suspected that I might as well have written nonsense syllables for all the difference it would make to the success of the show. For you, the reader, your loss is my gain: you can't hear the tunes, but I get the satisfaction of knowing that, for once, you got the words.

18 Wheels

Preface

Call it a machine, call it a beast, call it a kind of a hand
For it becomes an extension of the man
When it roars it's we together are the lion:
And we live long like lions
                                    often moving, often waiting
                                    years to pounce.

                    —Milton Acorn, *Riding With Joe Hensby*

In the spring of 1975, the actor Booth Savage suggested that we put a show together about truck drivers. Initially it was thought that the show would be constructed the way all Theatre Passe Muraille vehicles were constructed at the time: a group of actors would perform the functions of researcher, playwright, performer and, often, director, all at once.

It was a technique that went back to *The Farm Show*, in which a group of actors researched and assembled a show about a southern Ontario farming community, then performed it before that community in Ray Bird's barn. The piece consisted mainly of monologues, assembled from taped interviews with the citizens and performed onstage in an often uncanny display of mimicry. These speeches were interspersed with mimed local activities from the alternative theatre repertoire, and with songs written by some hapless composer like myself. *The Farm Show* was a real watershed at the time, and it still holds up well onstage, a kind of manifesto that demonstrates in microcosm the Paul Thompson vision of the theatre as a place where a group of people gather to contemplate their collective reflection.

A number of shows were assembled in the Seventies using this technique, and its limitations became obvious very quickly as the limitations of the documentary form. Found objects tend to be inflexible and result in linear, variety show structures with imagery that is strictly single entendre. And there is always a preponderance of functional language that fulfills the need for information and meaning the way concrete fills a hole. More than anything, though, the process tended to drive actors crazy.

Rehearsals tended to go on for months, and took place in shabby, often unheated buildings. I remember demoralized, exhausted, terrified actors in their winter coats improvising scene after scene, speech after speech, frantically groping for a story, a theme, any handhold at all, while Thompson performed the role of cheerleader, group psychologist and ideologist, firmly believing in the creative potential of anarchy, resolutely refusing to come to any conclusions until the last possible moment. Months of waltzing on the edge of the abyss can unhinge anyone, and at times it was sheer bedlam. Finally the show was thrown together in a blind panic a few days before opening. On opening night there were scene lists taped to the back of the scenery and, even as the house lights dimmed, pairs of perspiring actors could be seen gathering in corners, frantically working on bits of dialogue that they would be performing before a paying audience in a matter of moments.

I don't think there was a single actor who didn't finish a production swearing never, never to work with Thompson again, but they always did. As soon as they went on to other things, actors discovered just how uncreative and suffocating the Canadian theatrical scene can be. Compared not to God, but to the competition, Thompson became a shining knight of vision and integrity, and in fact his excruciating process developed an exceptionally creative generation, too creative for most of our directors. One production I worked on featured David Fox, Claire Coulter, Eric Peterson, Anne Anglin, Miles Potter, Booth Savage, Ted Johns and Janet Amos, all working for Equity minimum.

But by the time I joined Theatre Passe Muraille ("joined" isn't the right word, it was more vague that that), Thompson was beginning to realize that the playwright does have a place in the theatre, and was exploring ways to integrate the playwright into the developmental process, most successfully with Rick Salutin in *1837: The Farmers' Revolt*. Thinking that this might be the route Savage and I would travel, Thompson agreed to produce our show about truck drivers, and committed a small amount of money to its development. Savage immediately set off in a truck to B.C. and back with a tape recorder, while I started writing songs about the Trans Canada Highway.

Weeks later, Savage returned with a vitamin deficiency and bad news. The life of a truck driver is a depressing litany of skull-reaming monotony, inhuman working conditions and hours, poor wages, bad food and debilitating physical complaints. He produced some coroners' reports on a terrible accident on Highway 400, thinking that they might have a certain Gothic appeal, then headed north on a more promising project with David Fox, Ted Johns and Eric Peterson, followed by a production of Hrant Alianak's *The Blues* in Vancouver. One of Canada's few leading men with masculinity, Savage was and is in greater demand than a theatrical songwriter with few credits and a dubious future.

But although the life of the truck driver defeated the documentary approach, for me the mythology of the man was a mother lode of metaphor, imagery, style and charisma, calling forth images of overpowered, chrome, fire-breathing dragons, piloted by tattooed loners who drove to the rhythms of Red Sovine and communicated on Citizen's Band radios in a language nobody else could understand. For the popular songwriter, the truck driver myth has inspired a musical genre of surprising richness and variety that includes love ballads, Gothic and desperado narratives, rhythmic dance numbers and work songs. In the popular imagination the truck driver has taken on the cultural symbolism of the cowboy, the Don Quixote wanderer, the runaway and the blue collar hero.

It occurred to me that the truck driver was the person who roamed the spaces between places and people, which struck me as a particularly North American image, for North America is perpetually in transition, a state of mind defined by where it has been and where it is going rather than where it is. North America needs motion the way Asia needs continuity. India has its temples; we have our cars.

For me, the transition mentality is essential to mental health; that, and a sense of peripheral space.

On several occasions I have spent time working in Europe, and I have always been troubled by a peculiar form of claustrophobia that arises out of the knowledge that there is another city twenty miles away, and another after that, and another country beyond that, in all directions, for mile after mile. Somehow that awareness robs me of a sense of peripheral space that allows me to breathe, psychologically. I need the Northwest Territories, although I feel no urgent desire to explore them, and when a foreign icebreaker questions Canadian sovereignty in the North, that icebreaker is, in a sense, invading my brains.

Every country is a state of mind really, an accumulation of mental imagery. I'm not even certain that the imagery I'm talking about here is peculiarly Canadian, but I was in no position to worry about that when I was writing *18 Wheels*. It was good enough for me that the truck driver suggested first-hand insights, ideas that I had not seen before on television or in the movies, and a show that might be at home in a performance situation that existed because the public wanted it to, apart from the artificially-inseminated Canadian theatre.

18 Wheels takes a form straight out of a southern Ontario beer parlour. The performers make up a country-and-western band specializing in narrative ballads in a variety of country music genres. There are three "sets" ("Haulin' Chicken Guts" is an interval to allow for scene changes), each of which tells a story in a different musical genre.

The first set opens with an up-tempo anthem in Citizen's Band radio language, an exotic collection of metaphors that are best left unexplained, followed by a tour of Canada that introduces the theme of space and distance, first as geography, then as metaphor in the Chekhovian tale of Sadie, a much-admired waitress in a truck stop, whose character is based upon a charismatic waitress in the Kennel Restaurant in Sackville, New Brunswick, whom I worshipped for three years in the late Sixties.

"Night Driving" tells the story of a truck driver's collision with the Grim Reaper that led him to become an evangelical Christian. It is based on a famous tragedy south of Barrie, Ontario, on Highway 400, and on a truck drivers' periodical called *The Highway Evangelist*, whose obituary column is entitled "Silent Wheels," and which documents the truck drivers' spiritual struggles in their own words, often in naive poetry of strained rhyme and uncertain rhythm. Despite, or perhaps because of, the naivete of the publication, it has power. Nothing short of a bomb is as violent as a highway accident, and the Canadian highway system is a killing-ground, a fact that the truck driver knows better than anyone, that makes heroic his seemingly mundane concern with safety. The tragedies these men witness are enormous, and their attempt to bridge the gap between what they see and what they can express has a lot of dignity. I tried to capture this in "Night Driving," with only partial success. Musically, this set is based on the *Phantom 309* Gothic ballad, and upon the film sound tracks of Ennio Morricone.

"Lloyd and Molly" is a cautionary fable based on the painful love ballad that has been a Nashville mainstay for decades. It tells of a small domestic tragi-comedy, but the story is also a broad allegory about Canada and about Canadians' attitudes to one another over time and distance, in the shadow of our more charismatic neighbour to the south. *18 Wheels* closes not with a bang, but with a lullaby that reiterates the themes of distance, separation and the spaces between us all.

I completed the words and music in late 1976, and the ever-flexible Paul Thompson committed Theatre Passe Muraille to a production, provided that I was willing to produce, direct, arrange, play guitar and piano, set up a tour of southwest Ontario with Dianne English, and possibly drive the truck as well. Frank Moore, Anne Anglin, Bob Haley and Ed Henderson agreed to perform for very little money, and Paul Williams designed an ingenious set that incorporated a huge truck made of bent aluminum conduit piping that could be disassembled and thrown into the back of a truck on tour. David Fox lent me his Volkswagen van. In mid-January we headed for the snow belt, where we performed in eight towns, with varying success.

18 Wheels opened at the Theatre Passe Muraille space in Toronto in February, 1977, and received mixed notices. The *Toronto Star* critic disliked the show's intentional naivete, its irony, and saw its self-mockery as an insult to the people portrayed. This is typical of the urban aesthete, elaborately protective of the rural comrades he knows nothing about, anxious to shield them from anything like a sense of irony, suspicious on their behalf of humour other than the *Hee Haw* variety. I don't agree with this approach: in fact, if there is an epidemic of humourless preciousness spreading across the land, and I think there is, the main carriers are to be found in our major centres, and in our cultural institutions.

After the run at Passe Muraille, *18 Wheels* received a production by Tamahnous Theatre in Vancouver, British Columbia. The show seemed to suit the prevalent temper, and it had two successful runs in Vancouver and a tour of British Columbia. As far as I was concerned, my first musical had enjoyed as good a hearing as any first effort had any right to expect, and I concentrated on *Billy Bishop Goes to War*.

In the summer of 1978, however, Richard Ouzounian decided to produce and direct *18 Wheels* as part of his first season as Artistic Director of Festival Lennoxville. The show set box office records there, largely because it managed to draw French-speaking audiences from Sherbrooke who enjoyed the music and the mythology of "les camioneurs." I wasn't aware of it at the time, but Ouzounian had created a bandwagon which was eagerly caught by the regional theatres, for the now-famous cutbacks had begun to take hold, and box office receipts were taking on an unprecedented significance. I was busy touring *Billy Bishop*, and my first show was history as far as I was concerned, but I did appreciate the royalty cheques.

I didn't always appreciate the productions. Regional theatres are usually greenhouses for breeding that superior sensibility, the urban aesthetic, and the show's sense of irony was often lost on producers. They tended to take the serious parts too seriously, and the humorous parts too lightly, with the result that the show often looked more stupid than it really is. I had come a long way with *Billy Bishop*, and was painfully aware of the shortcomings of *18 Wheels*, but even so, the I.Q. of the show isn't nearly as low as some of its productions made it out to be, and there were times when I felt like standing up in the theatre, shouting: "No! Stop! That isn't it at all!", like a parody of an outraged playwright.

I'm more sanguine now. I watch the show in one of its forty-odd incarnations with fond detatchment, like an old friend who is acting a bit silly, but whom one loves just the same. It would be nice if theatre directors were a bit more aware of the music people actually listen to on their radios, if they were a bit less enamoured with the Broadway melodies of Steven Schwartz and Sondheim, but the Canadian audience is a forgiving bunch, grateful for any shred of familiarity they can find on a stage that is usually as alien to them as Kabuki.

Sometimes it is not the production but my own writing that makes me wince. My musical and literary taste is different now, and I find *18 Wheels* to be a little too reliant on folk stereotypes. I wish its aim were a little more precise, and all that rhyming begins to wear on me, all that intentional naivete. But when I imagine the piece not as drama but as performance art, and when I pretend that it was written by someone else, then I find it quite refreshing, and I remind myself that it has given pleasure to several people over the years. After all, *18 Wheels* was my first. We are all very fond of our firsts, for their imperfections. The first one is always the hardest; it always shows the writer at his most vulnerable.

18 Wheels was originally produced by Theatre Passe Muraille, and starred Frank Moore, Robert Haley and Anne Anglin. Scenery and lighting were designed by Paul Williams, with musical accompaniment by Ed Henderson and John Gray, and stage management by Dianne English. The playwright/composer would like to acknowledge the contributions and encouragement of Booth Savage, Paul Thompson and Pamela Hill.

18 Wheels

Characters

JIM, a lead singer brimming with masculine charm and charisma.

SADIE, a voluptuous female Country and Western singer.

MOLLY, a willowy female singer and comedienne with large, luminous eyes.

LLOYD, a male singer and comedian, preferably overweight.

JIM, SADIE, MOLLY and LLOYD are front-line performers for a Country and Western band. Each singer performs one principal role and a variety of minor roles, backed by a guitar, bass, drums and, if possible, a steel guitar. The musicians also assume roles at times, usually speaking in unison.

Setting

The principal visual element is a representation of at least the cab of a semi truck, a working truck as opposed to an elaborate show truck, but splendid nonetheless. The truck must be capable of a transformation in which it becomes a set representing a truck stop restaurant.

Around this central unit are the musical instruments, microphones, monitor speakers, and all the other paraphernalia associated with a performance by a Country and Western band.

Songs

"That CB Radio"	The Company
"Do You Wanna Know the Country"	Sadie & Molly
"Star of the Hollywood Grille"	Jim & Lloyd
"And All My Friends Said"	Sadie
"That's When Her Heart Broke Down"	Sadie, Jim & Lloyd
"Haulin' Chicken Guts"	Lloyd
"Life and Death"	Molly
"Night Driving"	Jim
"Silent Wheels"	Jim, Sadie & Molly
"Ridin' With Jesus"	The Company
"Times Are Tough"	Lloyd & Molly

"Bet You Won't Be Lonesome"	Lloyd
"You Know I Always Loved You"	Molly
"Partners"	Lloyd & Molly
"Campfire Theme"	The Band (whistled)
"Procter & Gamble"	Molly & Sadie
"Molly"	Lloyd, Sadie & Jim
"On the 401"	The Company

Act One

Do You Wanna Know the Country

The band plays a rhythmic, throbbing introduction. We hear a semi truck rev up its engine and take off down the highway with a loud roar. A spotlight hits JIM, who sings the first verse of "That CB Radio":

Well breaker ten it's the Duke again
C'mon, c'mon, Big Chief
I'm just behind, I'm runnin' blind
With a reefer of swingin' beef
And I see you got that parking lot
You're off to Buffalo
You shake the trees, I'll rake the leaves
With that CB radio
C'mon.

Another spotlight hits LLOYD, who sings the second verse:

Well here's the Chief, it's my belief
We got a big ten-four
You're lookin' clear, now you got ears
And I'm your big front door
If I see them bears sittin' anywhere
I will let you know
Commit no crime, we'll make good time
With that CB radio
C'mon.

MOLLY and SADIE join JIM and LLOYD for the chorus:

Well mercy guy, c'mon, c'mon
Won't you put that hammer down
Let's put on steam while it's all clean
And there ain't no bears around
Yeah, mercy guy, c'mon, c'mon
Won't you let that hammer go
You shake the trees, I'll rake the leaves
With that CB radio
C'mon.

JIM:
  Well breaker ten it's the Duke again
  You know I'd appreciate
  If you'd make a loop 'round that chicken coop
  I'm a little bit overweight

LLOYD:
  Well here's the Chief to bring relief
  Let's take the old two-oh
  Threes on you we'll make it through
  With that CB radio.

COMPANY:
  Well mercy guy, c'mon, c'mon
  Won't you put that hammer down
  Let's put on steam while it's all clean
  And there ain't no bears around
  Yeah, mercy, guy, c'mon, c'mon
  Won't you let that hammer go
  You shake the trees, I'll rake the leaves
  With that CB radio
  C'mon.

JIM:
  Well breaker ten it's the Duke again
  And we're comin' into Buffalo
  I see a bear sittin' in the air
  We'd better take it slow
  Chief I thank you for your good front door
  It's time for me to go
  But I'll hear you on the flip-flop
  With that CB radio.

COMPANY:
  Well mercy guy, c'mon, c'mon
  Won't you put that hammer down
  Let's put on steam while it's all clean
  And there ain't no bears around
  Yeah, mercy, guy, c'mon, c'mon
  Won't you let that hammer go
  You shake the trees, I'll rake the leaves
  With that CB radio.

The song ends. JIM, LLOYD, MOLLY and SADIE address the audience.

JIM: You know, some people say Canada's a farm in Ontario.
SADIE: Some say it's the Northland, just a heap of snow.
LLOYD: Some say it's a shopping centre in suburban Montreal.
MOLLY: Some see it in a maple tree in Nova Scotia in the fall.
JIM: Twenty million Canadas, each one is the best.
SADIE: Everybody's Canada seems to discount all the rest.
LLOYD: But you won't find Canada in B.C. or Prince Edward Isle.
MOLLY: You'll find it on a concrete river, stretchin' out a million
  miles.

*During the last two speeches, the band has been playing an introduction
to "Do You Wanna Know the Country." SADIE and MOLLY sing,
seductively:*

  Do you wanna know the country
  Get your ass out on the road
  Get on that concrete river
  Watch it as it flows
  Over space and time and distance
  A million miles or more
  This country is a highway
  Stretchin' out from shore to shore.

  Do you wanna know the country
  Then just ask the man
  Who knows that concrete highway
  Like the back of his hand
  He knows what it looks like
  He knows how it feels
  The man who knows the country
  Is the man on 18 wheels.

The band begins a rhythm change. The following is performed as a recitative.

JIM:
  He can be out there on a flatbed
  With fifty tons of logs
  Or drivin' a cabover
  With a reefer full of hogs.

LLOYD:
  In a 1950 Mack Truck
  With a suicide box in back
  Or a custom-built Kenworth
  Called a country Cadillac.

JIM:
> With torpedos and Budd Wheels
> Flashing coloured lights
> Six hundred-power Cummins
> Roarin' through the night.

LLOYD:
> That truck can be a Jonas
> That can kill you twenty ways
> Or a pussycat with a woman's name
> Proudly on display.

JIM:
> He got a dogbox, an auxbox
> Sixteen forward gears
> That man don't touch that clutch
> Gearjammers use their ears.

SADIE and MOLLY sing a reprise of "Do You Wanna Know the Country":

> Get out on that Highway
> Hear that engine roar
> And you're gonna see a country
> That you've never seen before
> Yeah, you're gonna see a Canada
> You've never seen . . .

The music abruptly launches into a fast, trucking rhythm in a minor key. The following is spoken as a recitative, to a strict, foot-tapping rhythm:

JIM:
> Take that truck through B.C.
> Up the mountain far as Hope
> Where that highway's just a two-lane
> On thirty to forty slope
> On your right a wall of green
> Those B.C. cedar trees
> Before you're done you'll see more wood
> Than you ever cared to see
> Got to mind the shoulders
> Got to keep your head
> You get a right front blowout, boy
> You're just as good as dead

Way into spring that highway's
Covered up with snow and ice
Take a look down the cliff, you'll see
The ones who paid the price
Four and eighteen-wheelers
At the bottom, gone to rust
No way to get them out of there
Just let them turn to dust
All you gotta do is miss one gear
You got a runaway
Your brakes burn out in seconds
All you do is pray
For a runaway road off the main
About thirty-five degrees
To take you to a dead-end stop
Crashin' through those Goddamned trees . . .
And all that time you'll get no sleep
You better take some pills
It's sure a welcome sight to see
Those green Alberta hills.

There is a key change, and the rhythm continues as before.

LLOYD:
Go truckin' through the prairie
Where the road's so straight and flat
You can drive a whole day, without
Knowin' where you're at
You're drivin' on a table underneath that prairie sky
And the rhythm of the prairie makes a deadly lullaby
'Cause when you can't see nothin'
But sky and grass and concrete
Your head gets heavy, eyes get dull
It's easy to go to sleep
So take a Bennie if you got any
Turn up that radio
In a couple of days you'll be so sick of trees
In Northern Ontario
That'll you'll long for that open feeling
Of that great big prairie sky
When you've seen five hundred miles of those
Goddamned trees . . .
You can watch the rocks go by.

There is a key change, and the rhythm continues.

SADIE:
    Go truckin' past Toronto
    Hear the city growl and grumble
    Six-lane commuter frenzy
    Through cloverleaf and tunnel
    See through the haze the golden towers
    Of corporate ambition
    Look at all the pretty lights
    Lit by nuclear fission.

MOLLY:
    Then you're truckin' through Quebec
    Through miles of little towns
    In the fall the leaves of red and orange
    Are burning all around
    Then you hit northern New Brunswick
    And what do you think you see
    Hundreds of miles, nothing but
    More of those Goddamned trees
    When you don't see any trees out front
    You're on the Atlantic coast
    So take the ferry to Newfoundland
    You'll get an overdose.

JIM:
    Do that trip about twenty times
    You might get to know this place
    Only through a windshield
    Can you see the country's face.

There is a key and rhythm change, as SADIE and MOLLY sing a reprise of "Do You Wanna Know the Country."

    Take a plane it ain't the same
    You're only in the air
    Starin' at your TV set
    You ain't been anywhere

Get out on that highway
Hear that engine roar
And you're gonna see a country
You've never seen before
Yes, you're gonna see a Canada
You've never seen . . .

The band abruptly plays the opening riff to "That CB Radio," which it continues to vamp as JIM and LLOYD, in spotlights, perform the following exchange, using their microphones as though they were CB radios.

JIM: Breaker for an eastbounder here's the Duke, you got a copy for me on this here seventeen, c'mon?

LLOYD: You got the Fox there Duke, you're lookin' clear back to the five nine six, but you got a bear in the grass with a picture taker next the chicken coop, and he's definitely eyeballin' the westbound lane, c'mon?

JIM: Ten-four there good buddy, mercy sakes alive we'll sure back off the hammer there at the five nine six, threes on you, we're on the side.

LLOYD: Don't feed any of the bears there, guy, keep the sunny side up and the dirty side down and we'll catch you on the flip-flop. Threes on you. We're on the side. Bye-bye.

The lights come up full as the Company sings a final verse of "That CB Radio."

Well mercy guy, c'mon, c'mon
Won't you put that hammer down
Let's put on steam while it's all clean
And there ain't no bears around
Yeah, mercy, guy, c'mon, c'mon
Won't you let that hammer go
You shake the trees, I'll rake the leaves
With that CB radio
You shake the trees, I'll rake the leaves
With that CB radio.

The song ends. Blackout.

Star of the Hollywood Grille

The truck has become the Hollywood Grille, a greasy truck stop somewhere in Alberta. LLOYD is seated at the counter, smoking and staring vacantly into space because it is 4 a.m. and he hasn't slept in recent memory.

The band is playing the "Campfire Theme" from Lloyd and Molly. *A guitar is being played in a desultory fashion, and there is some whistling.*

Enter JIM, who is in worse shape than LLOYD is. He sits beside LLOYD. They don't acknowledge one another's presence right away, and there is a pause as they stare in space. The band plays on.

LLOYD: Jim.

Pause.

JIM: Lloyd.

Pause.

LLOYD: Makin' her pay?
JIM: Who can make her pay, Lloyd? Who? Who's paying? *Pause.* What am I talking about?

Pause.

LLOYD: You drivin' all night, then?

Pause.

JIM: Yup.

LLOYD checks his watch.

LLOYD: I make it 4 a.m. What time you start?

Jim tries very hard to remember.

JIM: Not sure, Lloyd.

Pause. LLOYD giggles at a joke that has occurred to him. JIM watches him with suspicion, for he is on speed and therefore slightly paranoid.

LLOYD: My wife, she says to me this morning, she says: "What are you haulin'?" "What're you haulin'," she says to me. And I say to her, I say: "A load of Vaseline for the Virgin Islands!"

LLOYD finds his joke very funny. JIM watches him, very paranoid.

LLOYD: Get it? A load of Vaseline for the Virgin Islands! *He laughs.*

JIM does his best to understand what LLOYD is talking about, then gives up. LLOYD finally stops laughing and becomes slightly morose. Both stare into space.

JIM: Bad wind about fifty mile back.

Pause.

LLOYD: Yup.

Pause.

JIM: You drivin' all night, then?

LLOYD: Yup.

Enter SADIE in a waitress' uniform.

SADIE: How long you guys been out here? Gee, I'm sorry to keep you waitin' like that.
LLOYD: Sadie.
JIM: Sadie.
SADIE: How you doin' Lloyd? Wow, Jim, you look like hell. What's the matter, you drivin' all night or somethin'? You runnin' late?
JIM: I'm always runnin' late, Sadie. Always.
SADIE: Everybody's runnin' late tonight. Don't you guys' bosses know it's snowin' outside?
LLOYD: Ain't snowin' in Florida, Sadie.

SADIE and LLOYD laugh at this. JIM tries and fails to get the point.

SADIE: What are you guys gonna eat, anyway?

LLOYD and JIM are a bit embarrassed at this question.

LLOYD: Just coffee, Sadie, just coffee. I, er, I ate a few miles back.
SADIE: Good to see you lookin' after your health, Lloyd. What about you, Jim?
JIM: I'm, I'm, I'm gonna have a . . . a banana split, with lots of nuts. Lots.
SADIE: Livin' it up, eh? OK, two coffees, one banana split.

For some reason, JIM finds this very funny. LLOYD and SADIE exchange concerned looks as SADIE exits. The band begins to play the introduction to "Star of the Hollywood Grille," a romantic ballad.

JIM: What were we talkin' about there?

LLOYD: *singing*
　It's a dirty old truck stop
　Somewhere in Alberta
　The boys always stop here to eat
　The spoons are all greasy
　The cooks are all sleazy
　The man at the cash is a cheat
　But the waitress who works on
　The twelve-to-eight shift
　The sight of her gives us a thrill
　Her name is Sadie
　A hell of a lady
　She's the star of the Hollywood Grille.

JIM:
　They give you a coffee
　Strong as fresh asphalt
　They call it hundred-mile brew
　It's made of old tar
　And ground up cigars
　And cooked for a decade or two
　But the waitress who gives you
　That unfragrant liquid
　Serves it with style and with skill
　Her name is Sadie
　A hell of a lady
　She's the star of the Hollywood Grille.

LLOYD & JIM:
　Sadie, the boys always loved you
　Sadie, the boys love you still
　Though far from your prime
　We think you're just fine
　You're the star of the Hollywood Grille.

SADIE enters and serves coffee as they sing.

　The stew is a nightmare
　The club sandwich worse
　The eggs are all shrivelled and dry
　The vegetables rotten
　The salad a curse
　The hamburger would make you cry
　But you eat and you smile

38

At the waitress who serves you
Though you know that you're going to be ill
Her name is Sadie
A hell of a lady
She's the star of the Hollywood Grille.

Sadie please tell us
What is the reason
Why you are languishing here
Why do you grace
This disgusting place
With your presence, year after year
Couldn't you find
A good restaurant
Before all your friends have been killed
We'd follow you, Sadie
A hell of a lady
The star of the Hollywood Grille.

Sadie, the boys always loved you
Sadie, the boys love you still
Though far from your prime
We think you're just fine
You're the star of the Hollywood Grille
You're the star of the Hollywood Grille.

*End song. JIM and LLOYD listen to SADIE, who tells her story to the
audience with lyrical musical accompaniment from the band.*

SADIE:
I was born in Stellarton, Nova Scotia
The dirtiest little coal town of them all
Dad worked in the mine
And we were doin' fine
The depression didn't bother us at all
My dad made lots of money in the Thirties
We had a house, we even had a phone
But when the mine gave out
There wasn't any doubt
Stellarton had a depression of its own.

Well by 1950, nobody was working
In 1951 we sold the car
Mom was scrounging dimes

39

And Dad was spending time
Drinking beer in the Legion bar
I was thirteen when I quit school
Got a job at the Caff waitin' on tables
But while I was washing dishes
I was wishing wishes
Dreams of leaving home when I was able.

SADIE sings, sweetly, like a little girl:

And all my friends said
Sadie you're so pretty
We'll see your picture in the paper someday
You'll be rich and famous in the city
Some Upper Canadian will steal your heart away.

I'd heard it's another world in Upper Canada
The people drink brandy with their tea
The days are always sunny
The people all have money
Upper Canada: that's the place for me
I made my plan when I met Stan from Cape Breton
A trucker with Bill Hanes from Bible Hill
Stan had seen the world
And I was just a girl
Being with Stan sure gave me a thrill.

Stan sure wasn't too good looking
I don't think he was even very smart
But Stan was seventeen
Thought I was a teenage queen
That trucker loved me with all his heart
Stan sometimes got a run to Upper Canada
I think that's what attracted me to him
It sure wasn't romance
I just wanted the chance
To wash that dirty coal dust from my skin.

SADIE sings, sweetly but determined:

And all my friends said
Sadie you're so pretty
We'll see your picture in the paper someday
You'll be rich and famous in the city
Some Upper Canadian will steal your heart away.

Then one day Stan got a run to Toronto
I packed my bags and then I said good-bye
I said, "Good-bye, Stellarton
You sure weren't any fun
I'm gonna wash that coal dust from my eyes"
In two days we arrived in Toronto
I opened the door and said, "Why thank you, Stan
Thanks for taking me along
Now I'll say so long
You're a nice guy, I hope you understand."

Well Stan's poor heart was broken
I could tell that he was just about to cry
But I was just a girl
And I was seeing the world
So I kissed him once, and then I said good-bye
I got a job as a waitress in Toronto
Waiting for my chance to come along
I would soon be rich
This was Ontario, wasn't it
Soon I realized that something was wrong.

SADIE sings, bitterly:

And all my friends said
Sadie you're so pretty
We'll see your picture in the paper someday
You'll be rich and famous in the city
Some Upper Canadian will steal your heart away.

I met a man with a pencilled moustache
Who introduced me to bad company
That man was a brute
In a hundred-dollar suit
And somehow, he made a slut of me
I was with a hundred men from Upper Canada
They were experts at the runaround
At first they amused me
Then I saw how they'd used me
And that's when my heart . . . broke down.

There is a brief pause while we contemplate SADIE's fate, then abruptly, the band breaks into the introduction to "That's When Her Heart Broke Down," a fast rock number. SADIE becomes a rock singer in coloured light, singing and dancing with a backup chorus, played by the revitalized LLOYD and JIM.

SADIE:
I was a woman with a taste for better things
I was a woman of style and form

LLOYD & JIM: She was a woman.

SADIE:
A woman with furs and diamond rings
Inside a waitress' uniform

LLOYD & JIM: So sad.

SADIE:
But I gave that up, I found the cup
Was too bitter for me to taste
I realized there ain't no prize
That's worth the friends you waste

LLOYD & JIM: That's worth the friends you waste.

SADIE:
I had a man, his name was Stan
But I gave that man the air

LLOYD & JIM: So long, Stan.

SADIE:
For powder rooms and French perfume
And satin underwear

LLOYD & JIM: Oo-la-la.

SADIE:
But I paid the price, it wasn't nice
I wound up on the knee
Of paper men and fickle friends
Who made a slut of me.

LLOYD & JIM:
That's when her heart broke down
That's when her heart broke down

SADIE: Without a friend in town.

LLOYD & JIM:
That's when her heart broke down
That's when her heart broke . . .

SADIE: Down.
All my wishes turned to broken dishes
That there ain't no glue can mend

LLOYD & JIM: Crazy glue.

SADIE:
My heart was sick and tired
There ain't no use to pretend
That you're havin' fun when you're on the run
And there's no one you can trust

LLOYD & JIM: In God we trust.

SADIE:
I began to cry and I wondered why
My plans had turned to dust.

LLOYD & JIM:
That's when her heart broke down
That's when her heart broke down

SADIE: Without a friend in town.

LLOYD & JIM:
That's when her heart broke down
That's when her heart broke . . .

SADIE: Down.

The band changes tempo and rhythm to a fast country swing shuffle.
SADIE speaks in rhythm:

So I settled in Alberta
Somehow it reminded me of home
Got a job as a waitress
The only life I've ever known
In this truck stop, that's because a trucker
Was once a friend to me
Now I like being near truckers
They appeal to me
They've got no class, grab your ass
But they've got a heart that's true
Truckers are mostly honest men

Don't tell lies to you
They know this truck stop's rotten
And the food we serve is swill
But it's me those truckers come to see . . .
I am the star of the Hollywood Grille.

*The band changes tempo and rhythm, as JIM and LLOYD sing a reprise
of "Star of the Hollywood Grille."*

It's a dirty old truck stop
Somewhere in Alberta
The boys always stop here to eat
The spoons are all greasy
The cooks are all sleazy
The man at the cash is a cheat
But the waitress who works on
The twelve-to-eight shift
The sight of her gives us a thrill
Her name is Sadie
A hell of a lady
She's the star of the Hollywood Grille.

Sadie, the boys always loved you
Sadie, the boys love you still
Though far from your prime
We think you're just fine
You're the star of the Hollywood Grille
You're the star of the Hollywood Grille.

End song. Lights fade to black.

Haulin' Chicken Guts

This song, which serves as an entre-act while the stage is set for "Night Driving," is sung by LLOYD, with JIM, SADIE and MOLLY singing backup. The band is in a bluegrass mode.

LLOYD:
   Well I been haulin' merchandise
   For nearly twenty years
   I haul steel and wood and cows
   Rocks and glass and beer
   But this load in back's the lowest of the low
   The humiliation that I feel
   No one will ever know-wo.

   The economy's collapsin'
   Everyone's in debt
   In times like these a trucker's
   Gotta take when he can get
   But right now I'd accept a welfare cheque
   The load I've got in back's
   An albatross around my ne-eck.

ALL:
   He's haulin' chicken guts
   In the hot August sun

LLOYD:
   Livin' like an outcast
   Scorned by everyone
   There ain't no romance
   There ain't no fun
   When you're haulin' chicken guts
   In the hot August sun.

   Colonel Sanders looks so clean
   In his linen suit so white
   We're all stuffed with his chicken
   And we're gruntin' with delight
   Well I got the leftovers in back
   The aroma in my cab's enough to cause a cardiac.

The smell ain't nothin' like
Kentucky Fried
The sun does nasty things
To a chicken that has died
It's a Canadian balance of trade
The Colonel gets the money
I get chicken guts, decayed.

ALL:
He's haulin' chicken guts
In the hot August sun

LLOYD:
Livin' like an outcast
Scorned by everyone
There ain't no romance
And pleasures there are none
When you're haulin' chicken guts
In the hot August sun.

I drive my truck and curse my fate
So lonely and so blue
In the taverns of the nation
My presence is taboo
My friends are repulsed by my bouquet
You can smell a Yankee sellout
A hundred miles away-yay.

While the Colonel's in Kentucky
Savourin' his wealth
The stench is gettin' worse up here
I'm fearin' for my health
It's a fact the public's never understood
Someone's got to haul the parts
That ain't so finger-lickin' good.

ALL:
He's haulin' chicken guts
In the hot August sun

LLOYD:
  Livin' like an outcast
  Scorned by everyone
  There ain't no romance
  There ain't no fun
  When you're haulin' chicken guts
  In the hot August sun.

End song. Blackout.

Act Two

Night Driving

The band plays the intro to "Life and Death." It is very mysterioso. In a single spotlight, MOLLY sings:

  You take it all so casual
  Second nature to you now
  You drive away, assuming
  That you'll make it back somehow
  Life and death, life and death
  That's the rhythm of the drum
  The name of the game
  That is played by everyone.

  You take it all so casual
  Who is in that car ahead
  Is he crazy, is he drunk
  In a flash you could be dead
  Life and death, life and death

Who has any power
When you're out there playing chicken
At a hundred miles an hour.

Take these worries from your mind
Thoughts of life and death
Watch the road and take your time
It's all a moment of life . . .
And death.

So you pass that car so close
You can smell that fellow's breath
Yeah, we take it all so easy
When it comes to life and death
Life and death, life and death
Sometimes it's such a shame
Life is sweet but any moment
Death could call your name.

Take these worries from your mind
Thoughts of life and death
Watch the road and take your time
It's all a moment of life . . .
And death.

Where are you driving
What's on your mind
What's your destination
Where's the end of the line
Life and death, who's counting
What's the measure of a lifetime . . .

You listen to the radio
You tap the wheel in time
The sun is shining down
You've got no worries on your mind
Life and death, life and death
The wheels are turning just the same
Whether or not we know how
Everybody plays the game.

Take these worries from your mind
Thoughts of life and death
Watch the road and take your time
It's just a moment of life
And death.

We hear a large semi revving up and taking off down the highway, settling into the steady rhythm of a truck cruising at sixty miles an hour. The band vamps the introduction to "Night Driving." The truck's headlamps shine directly at the audience, and between them is the face of JIM as JAMES NEW, illuminated eerily by the pale dashboard light.

JAMES NEW:
My name is James New, I'm thirty years of age
I work for Kingsway Trucking, driving for a wage
Heading out to Winnipeg on Highway 17
Drive all night while traffic's light
That's my routine
Used to be an independent
Now those days are gone
Sometimes when I'm driving late at night
I sing this song.

He sings:

On a black November night
It's stark and cold
And I'm driving through the night
Like some lost soul
The pills I take keep me awake ,
But I'm higher than a kite
Goin' down the road, haulin' my load
All night.

One thing that I've never understood
In the darkness nothing looks the way it should
The hands on the wheel in front of me
Glow green in the acid light
Goin' down the road, haulin' my load
All night.

Chorus
It's like we're always living on that highway
Where the night is all around
As thick as clay
And death is riding shotgun all the way, now
Death is riding shotgun all the way.

The music stops. We hear the truck driving along.

JAMES NEW: Driving all night, there's nothing to do but think.

*Music: Theme 1: Ominous. The other actors narrate the following as
JAMES NEW drives. The effect should be as though this is all a memory
passing through his head.*

MOLLY:
His name was Charles Caccia
And he drove a red Pinto
Heading south, near Barrie
Sailing through the wind and snow
In an awful hurry
Got to get to Toronto
Driving down Highway 400.

LLOYD:
I was passing this green sedan
When all at once I couldn't see
The highway became
A wall of snow in front of me
As the car began to spin I cursed
My stupidity
A whiteout on Highway 400.

SADIE:
They got out of their cars
To make sure everyone's all right
But they couldn't see a thing
The whole world had turned to white
Then a crash, and then another
And faces froze in fright
A pileup on Highway 400.

Music: Theme 2: Heavy, crashing rock.

LLOYD:
Then a tractor trailer full of lumber
Thundered through the snow
He tried to stop, but on the ice
It was plain where he would go
He jackknifed and plowed into
Four cars in a row
That was just the start on Highway 400
Then a bus came tearing through the white
With a sick, metallic noise
Some cars were crushed like tissue
Others bounced around like toys
The truck and trailer overturned
And nearly fifty tons
Of lumber came crashing down
Trapping everyone
Then the gas tanks started to blow
And the fire began to spread
The people trapped beside the truck
Were just as good as dead.

Music continues. We see the reflection of fire behind the illuminated face of JAMES NEW.

MOLLY:
You could hear people screaming
As the fire lit the sky
"Help me, please, I'm burning!"
But no one dared to try
You had to save who you could
And leave the others left to die
And there was lots of death on Highway 400.

The gas tanks kept exploding
The deadly furnace burned
For over sixty people
A Sunday drive had turned
Into a nightmare out of hell
And all those people learned
About violent death on Highway 400.

SADIE:
  For hours the only injured
  Helped the nearly dead
  People moaned with broken backs
  Blood ran dark and red
  It was a scene out of a war
  Or a nightmare in your head
  It was like a bomb had dropped on Highway 400.

LLOYD:
  They pried children from the twisted metal
  Of the family car
  They pulled a woman in a bloody fur coat
  Out of her Jaguar
  And every one of the survivors
  Will always have the scars
  Of that white Sunday on Highway 400.

*The music stops. JAMES NEW is driving his truck. We hear the band
vamp the intro to "Night Driving" as he speaks.*

JAMES NEW:
  Even with the stereo tape
  And the CB radio
  The sound of the engine
  The speedometer's dim glow
  All I really have are thoughts
  To keep me company
  And it gets so hard to shut out
  All them painful memories
  Yes, it's easy to scare yourself
  This time in the morning
  Thoughts of life and death can come
  And hit you with no warning.

He sings:

  The highway takes a dive
  The headlights dance
  Life and death are playing
  Games of chance
  Red eyes that shine in front and behind
  Are a terrifying sight

Goin' down the road
Haulin' my load
All night.

Chorus
It's like we're always livin' on that highway
Where the night is all around, as thick as clay
And death is riding shotgun all the way, now
Death is riding shotgun all the way.

Music: Theme 1 but more lyrical than ominous now.

SADIE:
When the sirens stopped wailing
And the flames died down at last
It was time to count the dead ones
No easy task
To tell which cars were just wrecks
And which cars were the caskets
That held the dead of Highway 400.

MOLLY:
Some cars were so crushed
It was a foot from roof to floor
There weren't any windows
And you couldn't see a door
One look at some
And everybody knew for sure
No one had lived through Highway 400.

LLOYD:
They cut the roofs open
Just like sardine cans
With a crane on a front-end loader
They peeled the metal back, and
When those cars were open
Then the sad part began
For those who knew the dead of Highway 400.

They looked inside at what was left
And there was hardly anything
A piece of bone, a pair of glasses
Perhaps a wedding ring

To remind us of those people
We heard call as they were dying
In that pile of flame on Highway 400.

Music stops. Silence. The actors share the following names.

John and Florence Johnson, with
A family of four
Jane and David Lewis
They added to the score
Fred Short and Susan Reese
Were engaged to be married
Eileen Jones and Peter Leafoot
Were in another car that carried
David Aikens and George Johnson
Who accompanied them in death
And a total of twelve people
Had taken their last breath
In that moment on Highway 400.

The band vamps the intro to "Silent Wheels," gently.

JAMES NEW:
Right about now I start wondering
If this night's ever gonna end
Wondering if I'll ever see
The light of day again
But I'm still on that yellow highway
And I'm sort of in control
I play a sad song on the tape deck
As I hear those big wheels roll
There's a cheap hotel in Winnipeg
I'll sleep when I arrive
Thoughts of what's gone by
Let me know I'm still alive.

He sings "Silent Wheels." The other actors sing backup.

Sometimes, when I'm driving late at night
I see the faces of dear friends who passed away
A truck knows that life is cheap
When you're on the road
He sees more death with every passing day.

If a plague killed as many
As die on that highway
Everyone would lock their doors in fear
But the people keep on dying
Their loved ones keep on crying
Just numbers to be counted every year.

Chorus
Silent wheels . . .
Rollin' through the afternoon of my life
Silent wheels . . .
Haunt me as I'm ridin' through my life
Some died without knowin'
Others died in pain
Silent wheels . . .
When will I see my friends again.

There was Earl who died in a fire in his cab
And George hit an underpass at night
Luke had a front-end blowout
And fifty tons of steel buried Jack
He died overnight.

But you can't tell a four-wheeler
Who thinks he knows it all
That the highway's the most violent place we know
He never gets the message
On the news each Sunday night
As the TV calmly counts the weekend toll.

Chorus
Silent wheels . . .
Rollin' through the afternoon of my life
Silent wheels . . .
Haunt me as I'm ridin' through my life
Some died without knowin'
Others died in pain
Silent wheels . . .
When will I see my friends again
When will I see my friends again.

The song ends. JAMES NEW is driving as before.

JAMES NEW:
My name is James New, and by now you probably know
I was the trucker in that accident years ago
I escaped without a scratch, but in my heart I know
I can't forget Highway 400.

I make my fifteen cents a mile
You won't believe this but it's true
I'm haulin' coffins to Winnipeg
In a couple of days they're due
So I'm driving all night long to get there
That's sure nothing new
And while I drive I think of Highway 400.

He sings the last verse of "Night Driving."

The darkness spins
Three hundred miles go by
Somehow I make it
Through the night alive
In an hour the icy sun
Will fill the road with pale grey light
Goin' down the road
Haulin' my load
All night.

Chorus
It's like we're always livin' on that highway
Where the night is all around, as thick as clay
And death is riding shotgun all the way, now
Death is riding shotgun all the way.

Key change. JAMES NEW sings a reprise of "Silent Wheels."

Silent wheels . . .
Rollin' through the afternoon of my life
Silent wheels . . .
Haunt me as I'm ridin' through my life
Some died without knowin'
Others died in pain
Silent wheels . . .
When will I see my friends again
When will I see my friends again.

Key change. LLOYD, SADIE and MOLLY hum the intro to "Ridin'
With Jesus." JAMES NEW sings as the morning sun comes up.

When the road is unfamiliar
And I think I've lost my way
Jesus is always there
To guide me when I pray
My windshield is clear again
My vision is restored
Ridin' with Jesus
Ridin' with the Lord.

Chorus
Ridin' with Jesus
Ridin' with a friend
And you know that Jesus always has
A helping hand to lend
Jesus doesn't ask much
It's a price you can afford
Ridin' with Jesus
Ridin' with the Lord.

Even though I'm all alone
His hands are at the wheel
The darkest road is brightened
By the light his truth reveals
And when my run is over
I'll be thankful he's aboard
Ridin' with Jesus
Ridin' with the Lord.

Chorus
Ridin' with Jesus
Ridin' with a friend
And you know that Jesus always has
A helping hand to lend
Jesus doesn't ask much
It's a price you can afford
Ridin' with Jesus
Ridin' with the Lord.

Ridin' with Jesus
Ridin' with the Lord.

End song, after repeats with key changes.

Act Three

Lloyd and Molly

Lights up with music. LLOYD and MOLLY sing "Times are Tough,"
a combative duet.

LLOYD:
  Oh my dad he loved my mom
  She was the finest in the land
  Went to call and brought her flowers
  Then he asked her for her hand
  When he came home she was waitin'
  With supper and a kiss
  She gave him seven children
  Forty years of wedded bliss.

  Chorus
  But times are tough for the man's man
  When his woman's got ideas he just don't understand
  Yes, times are rough for the man's man
  When he wakes one day to find his woman
  Gettin' out of hand.

MOLLY:
  Oh my mom gave up her life
  Just to give my dad a home
  Between the children and the house
  She had no time to call her own
  Time made her old
  With loneliness and drudgery
  Though I love them both, the life they had
  Ain't good enough for me.

  Chorus
  Oh you think you got it tough
  Bein' a woman takes its toll
  It's hard to love your life
  When someone else is in control
  Oh you think you got it tough

It's just like bein' on parole
When a woman takes a man sometimes
She's sellin' out her soul.

LLOYD & MOLLY:
Oh let's listen to this story
'Bout a wife who went astray
Try and understand how hard it is
To honour and obey
Try and share the pain
With the hero of this tale
And be kind to one another
We'll be lonely if we fail.

LLOYD and MOLLY sing the chorus together as counterpoint.

End song. The music punctuates the following, which is performed as a kind of story theatre, with LLOYD and MOLLY acting out the situations and incidents narrated by JIM and SADIE.

JIM:
Well the independent trucker
Never lives like normal folk
He's always on the road
And he's always nearly broke.

SADIE:
The cost of gas is risin', you know
It gets higher every year.

JIM:
Gettin' so you can't afford
To drive in second gear
Yes, the independent trucker
Never has an easy life.

SADIE:
But the one who has it harder
Is the independent's wife.

Lights up on LLOYD, dealing with the severe limitations of his old and battered truck while MOLLY looks on wistfully.

JIM:
Lloyd was an independent
He drove his truck alone

SADIE:
  And when he hit the road
  He always left his wife at home

JIM:
  Now Lloyd loved that woman dearly
  Molly was her name

SADIE:
  But Lloyd was never home
  And every year it was the same
  To make those payments he was workin'
  Seven days a week
  Sometimes it seemed like he was livin'
  In that driver's seat
  Molly would say:

MOLLY: *to LLOYD*
  Please take me with you
  I don't like it here alone

JIM:
  But Lloyd was from the old school

LLOYD: *to MOLLY*
  A woman's place is in the home.

With a masculine gesture, LLOYD gets into his truck as MOLLY gets into her apron and sets up a kitchen area containing a chrome-and-plastic table and two chairs.

JIM:
  Now Lloyd drove a '57 Mack truck
  A wreck without a doubt
  The grille was gone forever
  The stack was rusted out
  The cab was like a pigpen
  With a lumpy cot in back
  The speedometer was broken
  Of course the windshield was cracked
  But Lloyd was ambitious
  Someday he'd make a buck
  He'd be a big time operator
  And he'd own a fleet of trucks
  Lloyd would say:

60

LLOYD: *to MOLLY*
Just you wait, Molly
Someday I'll treat you right
We'll be rich, just have patience
It don't happen overnight.

SADIE:
Lloyd never noticed Molly
Showin' signs of strain

MOLLY shows signs of strain.

Because Molly was a strong one
And she never did complain
But somehow it seemed nothing
Ever went the way it should
Most of the time business
Just wasn't any good.

JIM:
Lloyd blamed it on monopolies
He said:

LLOYD:
Those Americans
Are ruining the country
For the Canadian businessman!

SADIE:
And Lloyd he cursed the government
And Lloyd he cursed the cops
He said:

LLOYD:
There's a conspiracy!
I'm the victim of a plot!

LLOYD beats his truck in despair.

SADIE:
Business got no better, though
No matter how he cursed
One year it was terrible
The next year it was worse.

Music stops. JIM steps forward and speaks sadly to the audience.

JIM:
　But no matter how bad the situation
　It can deteriorate
　And there just ain't no controllin'
　Those malicious wheels of fate.

JIM moves into the kitchen area as MOLLY's lover. MOLLY flings off her apron after a brief flirtation and falls into his arms. LLOYD, driving his truck, senses this as though by intuition.

SADIE:
　Molly was actin' strangely
　It wasn't long before Lloyd began
　To realize that Molly
　Was seein' another man.

Spot on LLOYD, who leans out of the window of his truck and sings "Bet You Won't Be Lonesome." JIM, SADIE and MOLLY sing backup. During the song, JIM and MOLLY conduct a kitchen romance, with MOLLY torn by guilt and infatuation.

　Another road
　Another run
　And the rain in my heart's just begun
　On the road alone now
　Got to leave you home now
　One more time.

　And I can see it
　In your eye
　It don't hurt you to say good-bye
　And when I'm drivin' lonely
　I can see that you'll be
　Doin' fine.

Chorus
　Bet you won't be lonesome
　I bet you won't be lonesome
　I can feel it
　In my bones some
　When I've been gone some
　Bet you won't be lonesome
　In the night

And the load
On my wheels
Got nothin' on the weight that I feel
Drivin' and a-thinkin'
Listen to the engine
Call your name

And I curse this old truck
I curse my life and my luck
Knowin' I should hate you
Knowin' that it ain't you
Who's to blame.

Chorus
Bet you won't be lonesome
I bet you won't be lonesome
I can feel it
In my bones some
When I've been gone some
Bet you won't be lonesome
In the night.

I'll be home
In a week
Dead tired 'cause I ain't had no sleep
And you'll smile and kiss me
And you'll say you miss me
Every day.

And I'll be
So damn glad
To be home, I missed you so bad
Maybe you really loved me
Maybe you really love me
In your way.

Chorus
But bet you won't be lonesome
I bet you won't be lonesome
I can feel it
In my bones some
When I've been gone some
Bet you won't be lonesome
In the night.

End song.

JIM:
One day Lloyd confronted Molly
He said:

LLOYD gets out of his truck, bursts into the kitchen area, and confronts MOLLY and JIM, who quickly slinks away.

LLOYD: *to MOLLY*
I understand
That while I've been on the road
You've been seein' another man!

SADIE:
Molly looked at him in silence

MOLLY does so.

Then she began to cry

MOLLY cries.

And when she'd pulled herself together

MOLLY pulls herself together.

This was her reply:

Music: Intro to "You Know I Always Loved You," a plaintive spoken ballad.

MOLLY: *speaking*
You know I always loved you
And I wanted to be true
But the days were so long and empty
I didn't know what I would do
I thought, if I have to spend one more night
Alone here in my room
With the house so dark and empty
As lonely as a tomb
Why I could just go crazy
And kill myself some day
That's why I took a lover
While you were away.

The song ends.

JIM:
Well on hearin' this Lloyd started thinkin'.

LLOYD thinks.

He began to feel ashamed

LLOYD feels ashamed.

He knew he must forgive her
'Cause he knew he shared the blame
Lloyd said:

Music to "You Know I Always Loved You" again. LLOYD speaks the ballad as MOLLY did, but with decisiveness and energy.

LLOYD:
Now listen, Molly
I'm gonna teach you how to drive
Lots of other truckers
Travel with their wives
So we'll always be together
And we'll never be alone
You and I'll be partners
This old Mack will be our home!

The music swells to a climax as LLOYD and MOLLY kiss. The music changes key and rhythm to a catchy riff as they get into the truck. LLOYD teaches MOLLY how to drive throughout the following, and she catches on fast. As she gets better the tempo of the music increases until we are into "Partners."

SADIE:
So Lloyd gave Molly lessons
How to steer and how to shift
And pretty soon he realized
That Molly had a gift
It was like she'd been born
With a gearshift in her hand
And it wasn't long before
She could drive just like man.

JIM:
Now Lloyd and Molly drove together
And it wasn't long before
Lloyd realized it was easier

With someone else to do the chores
They could drive around the clock
And the truck made better time
They got some brand-new contacts
And the business was lookin' fine

LLOYD and MOLLY sing.

Chorus
Oh we're partners
And we're livin' in a cab
We're partners in the good times
And partners in the bad
Two hearts meet on the driver's seat
And that's our rendezvous
We're partners and we're livin'
In a truck that's built for two
We're partners and we're drivin'
In a truck that's built for two.

LLOYD:
Yes we're drivin' to Toronto
With a wallet full of cash
Molly shifts those sixteen gears
Quicker than a flash
She can drive a week without no sleep
And still stay on the road
Yes it's good to have a partner
Someone to share the load.

MOLLY:
This cab is full of grease and dust
It never has been clean
The truck stops all are greasy spoons
The truckers are obscene
But I'd put up with twice as much
Before I'd go back home
'Cause it's better to be a partner
Than to go through life alone.

Chorus
Oh we're partners
And we're livin' in a cab
We're partners in the good times

And partners in the bad
Two hearts meet on the driver's seat
And that's our rendezvous
We're partners and we're livin'
In a truck that's built for two
We're partners and we're drivin'
In a truck that's built for two.

Music continues. JIM and SADIE speak over "Partners" music.

SADIE:
So they drove around for near a year
All over Canada
And Molly worked just like a dog
She sure had stamina.

JIM:
And every night Lloyd thanked the Lord
For givin' him his wife
Yes, it seemed Lloyd's luck was turnin'
For the first time in his life
That's right
It seemed Lloyd's luck was turnin'
For the first time in his life.

LLOYD & MOLLY: *singing*
Yes we're partners
And we're livin' in a cab
We're partners in the good times
And partners in the bad
Lloyd he is the captain
And Molly is the crew, a-ooo
We're partners and we're livin'
In a truck that's built for two
We're partners and we're drivin'
In a truck that's built for two.

End of song. The music stops. JIM and SADIE have a cautionary word with the audience.

JIM:
Now it's only human nature
When it comes to doin' work
When the goin' gets easier

It gets easier to shirk
And to let the others take a bit
Of your share of the load

SADIE:
And Molly was spending a lot more time
Driving down that road
While Lloyd was spending a lot more time
On the cot in back
It was pretty clear to anyone
That Lloyd was gettin' slack.

LLOYD has been lounging around the truck while MOLLY drives.

Now the music hits an ominous, minor chord. Lights dim. Perhaps a clap of thunder. SADIE and JIM are aware of the portents and flinch.

JIM:
Then came that awful morning
January twenty-four
When Fate clobbered Lloyd
Like it never had before
They had a load of iron
On a run from the Timmins mine
And with the snow and ice and wind
They were makin' lousy time.

MOLLY is driving, trying to see through snow, fog, etc. We hear the sound of heavy wind. LLOYD of course is lounging.

SADIE:
You could hardly see the road
And the windshield wipers froze
Molly had driven eight hours straight
Fatigue had begun to show
The morning of the day before was
The last time they had a meal
They'd have gone off the road if Molly weren't
A genius at the wheel.

JIM:
Now if Lloyd had been thinkin'
He'd have noticed somethin' wasn't right
For Molly hadn't uttered
A single word all night.

SADIE:
> Sometimes your closest friend's the last to see
> That something's on your mind
> And when it came to Molly's feelings
> Lloyd might as well have been blind
> On they drove, a hundred
> Dreary miles without a break
> And Lloyd was lost in thought about
> The money that he'd make.

JIM:
> They came upon a truck stop
> Molly said:

MOLLY:
> Let's catch our breath
> Let's have a cup of coffee before
> I drive myself to death.

The truck slows and stops along with the music. LLOYD and MOLLY mime the following sequence. The band plays a sexy blues number.

JIM:
> So they pulled into a parking lot
> Beside a Kenworth rig
> And beside Lloyd's old Mack that Kenworth
> Sure looked mighty big.

SADIE:
> With its candy-apple paint job
> Its chrome plated stacks
> A custom grille out front
> A hundred licence plates out back
> It was like a jewelled monster
> Gleaming chrome and candy red
> And in behind the driver's seat
> Was a great big double bed.

Ominous chord. LLOYD and MOLLY do takes, for different reasons.

JIM:
> Now the sight of that big Kenworth
> Was enough to make Lloyd squirm
> 'Cause on the door was the trademark
> Of a big American firm
> Lloyd said:

LLOYD:
  Those Americans
  Always get the big pay-loads
  Goddamn Yankee cowboys
  Think they own the road!

SADIE:
  But Molly didn't say anything
  She turned off the ignition key
  And then she said:

MOLLY:
  I'll check the tires
  You go in and order coffee.

JIM:
  Well that was fine with Lloyd
  'Cause it sure was cold out there
  Lloyd said:

LLOYD:
  You'll freeze your ass.

SADIE:
  And Molly said:

MOLLY:
  I don't care.

JIM:
  So Lloyd left the Mack
  Beside the Kenworth, red and gold
  And went in and ordered coffee.

SADIE:
  Leaving Molly in the cold.

LLOYD exits into the kitchen area which will become the cafe. MOLLY sings "Procter & Gamble."

  Work for him, work for him
  Cook him his meals
  Give him your loving
  Have sex appeal
  Give him an aspirin when he has the flu
  That's what you live for when you're number two
  That's what you live for when you're number two.

Chorus
But Procter & Gamble
Clean everything in sight
Downy will keep
Your towels soft and light
Linoleum rec rooms and string macrames
Hoover vacuums and Melmac for days.

The TV don't love you
The washer don't care
New paint won't brighten
A pallid affair
Hours and hours with nothing to do
That's what you live for when you're number two
That's what you live for when you're number two.

But Procter & Gamble
Clean everything in sight
Downy will keep
Your towels soft and light
Linoleum rec rooms and string macrames
Hoover vacuums and Melmac for days.

Molly exits. Lights up on the kitchen area which is now a cafe. LLOYD has been joined by members of the band and mimes the following. The band plays a whistled campfire tune.

JIM:
    Lloyd went into the truck stop
    Sat beside the stove's warm glow
    And recognized the faces
    Of some friends from long ago
    They all got to reminiscing 'bout
    Those old and happy times
    The coffee tasted good
    And old Lloyd was feelin' fine
    Quite a while went by
    They talked and laughed without a care
    Then Lloyd began to wonder
    Why Molly wasn't there
    Lloyd wondered:

LLOYD:
Where is that woman?
It sure is a damn cold night.

JIM:
But someone told another joke
And Lloyd thought

LLOYD:
She's all right.

JIM:
But half an hour went by
And Lloyd began to be concerned
When he got up and looked out the window
It was then Lloyd's stomach turned!

Ominous chord from the band as LLOYD reacts.

SADIE:
Lloyd saw his dingy Mack truck
Sittin' just where it had been
But Molly and the Kenworth
Were nowhere to be seen!

The band plays urgent music in a minor key.

SADIE:
Lloyd stood in frozen silence
Then he let out such a roar

LLOYD:
Aaaaaahhhhhhhhhhhhhhhhh!!

SADIE:
That a dozen startled coffee cups
Came crashing to the floor
Lloyd ran out without his coat
Into the wind and snow and cold

LLOYD does.

He found the Kenworth's tracks headin' south
And they weren't very old.

LLOYD points south. The band resumes playing the whistled campfire tune while watching the scene with curiosity.

JIM:
  The boys watched all this with interest
  For a good ten minutes or more
  Then one of them said he ain't seen Lloyd
  Act like this before

Urgent music in a minor key.

SADIE:
  Lloyd ran back into the truck stop.

LLOYD does.

  He said:

LLOYD:
  Any of you boys figure
  You know the fellow driving
  That great big Kenworth rig?

JIM:
  And the boys said:

BAND: *in unison*
  Uh, we don't know him
  But he left an hour ago
  He's a big, handsome American
  And he's headed for Buffalo!

JIM:
  Lloyd said:

LLOYD:
  Thanks a lot, boys
  That's all I want to hear
  I'm gonna catch that Kenworth
  If it takes me twenty years.

LLOYD mimes the following to urgent music, ending up in the Mack truck, driving furiously and singing.

SADIE:
  Lloyd went back to the Mack without saying good-bye
  And disconnected his load
  You could hear those tires screeching
  As he took off down the road.

The band plays the intro to "Molly," a very fast swing tune in the style of Bob Wills. LLOYD sings.

LLOYD:
 Well I paid a bitter price
 And that ain't nice

JIM & SADIE:
 Wa-waaa.

LLOYD:
 No one should be treated this a-way

JIM & SADIE:
 Too bad.

LLOYD:
 And if I ever find her
 I'm gonna treat her kinder
 I'll get down on my knees to make her stay.

JIM & SADIE:
 Waa-waaa.

LLOYD:
 Though I'm lonely, and this old truck's the only
 Friend I've got, I'd give it up to make her smile
 And I'm tellin' you, by golly
 I'm gonna find my Molly
 If I have to drive a million miles.

LLOYD, JIM & SADIE:
 Chorus
 Molly . . .
 Is out there on that highway
 Molly . . .
 Just up and ran away
 Molly . . .
 Is somewhere on that highway
 Molly . . .
 Went and made her getaway.

The band continues fast swing motif during the following narration. LLOYD mimes.

SADIE:
　　With knuckles white and jaw set tight
　　Lloyd headed for the south
　　He drove all day and all the night
　　His heart was in his mouth
　　He crossed the U.S. border
　　Doing ninety-five at least
　　And all the time his eyes were peeled
　　For that candy-apple beast.

JIM:
　　A couple of times he thought he saw
　　The Kenworth's big tail lights
　　But he couldn't be sure, and anyway
　　They soon were out of sight
　　The Mack flew into New York State
　　And into Buffalo
　　And Lloyd didn't have to wait
　　He knew just where to go.

SADIE:
　　He stomped into the head office
　　Of that big American line
　　With the name he saw on the Kenworth door
　　Displayed on a neon sign.

"Molly" continues.

LLOYD:
　　I hope and I pray I'm not too late

JIM & SADIE:
　　Waa-waaa.

LLOYD:
　　To bring that girl back home where she belongs

JIM & SADIE:
　　Atta boy.

LLOYD:
　　Since she left with that American
　　I'm feelin' like an also-ran
　　I'm yearnin' for her all day long

JIM & SADIE:
  Waa-waaa.

LLOYD:
  Drivin' this old heap I get no sleep

JIM & SADIE:
  Waa-waaa.

LLOYD:
  And cryin' bitter tears just ain't my style

JIM & SADIE:
  What a man.

LLOYD:
  And I'm tellin' you by golly
  I'm gonna find my Molly
  If I have to drive a million miles.

LLOYD, SADIE & JIM:
  Molly . . .
  Is out there on that highway
  Molly . . .
  Just up and ran away
  Molly . . .
  Is somewhere on that highway
  Molly . . .
  Went and made her getaway.

*The music stops dead. JIM dons an eyeshade and becomes the Chicago
DISPATCHER.*

SADIE:
  Lloyd told the Dispatcher what had happened.

LLOYD performs a synopsis of the story so far, in mime.

  The Dispatcher faked concern.
  He said:

JIM: *as DISPATCHER*
  Oh my, oh my, oh my
  How it distresses me to learn
  That one of our American boys
  Could do somethin' to offend
  'Cause you know how we all cherish
  Our dear Canadian friends.

LLOYD looks dubious.

SADIE:
  He said:

JIM: *as DISPATCHER*
  Yes! I know that driver
  That truck sure is a pearl
  I heard he took a partner
  And I heard it was a girl

LLOYD has a slight angina attack.

  I could of sworn that trucker
  Was the finest one alive
  But that girl that he got with him?
  Boy, can she ever drive!

The band plays violent music. LLOYD goes berserk according to the following:

SADIE:
  Oh hearing this, poor old Lloyd
  Near had a heart attack
  His hands went numb, his face went white
  He reeled and staggered back
  Then he jumped on that Dispatcher
  And he grabbed him by the neck
  He said:

LLOYD:
  That woman is my wife!
  I'm here to collect:
  Now if you know her whereabouts
  You'd better tell me, Boy!

SADIE:
  The Dispatcher choked and gagged and said:

JIM: *as DISPATCHER*
  They've gone to Illinois!
  They've gone to Chicago! They're on another run!
  Now please let go my neck
  'Cause I ain't havin' any fun!

The fast swing music resumes as LLOYD gets back into the truck and mimes the following, with great determination.

JIM:
   So Lloyd got up and left that man
   Lyin' on the floor
   Without apologizin'
   He ran straight out the door
   Lloyd made that poor old Mack truck
   Hop about just like a toy
   And without so much as a bite to eat
   Took off for Illinois!

"Molly" continues.

LLOYD:
   That dirty Yank is who I've got to thank

JIM & SADIE:
   Waa-waaa.

LLOYD:
   But it sure ain't revenge that's on my mind

JIM & SADIE:
   Love hurts.

LLOYD:
   I don't mean no harm
   I wanna take her in my arms
   And say I never meant to be unkind
   I'm haunted by the moon and stars at night

JIM & SADIE:
   Blue moon.

LLOYD:
   Rememberin' when I walked her down that aisle

JIM & SADIE:
   I do.

LLOYD:
   And I'm tellin' you by golly
   I'm gonna find my Molly
   If I have to drive a million miles.

   Molly . . .
   Is out there on that highway
   Molly . . .
   Just up and ran away

Molly . . .
Is somewhere on that highway
Molly . . .
Went and made her getaway.

The music stops dead. JIM once again plays the dispatcher.

SADIE:
　　The dispatcher in Chicago
　　Confirmed Lloyd's darkest fears.

JIM: *as DISPATCHER*
　　They got another contract
　　And they took off out of here
　　They've got a load of fridges
　　To take to New Mexico
　　They've been gone about a day now
　　And that's all I know.

Fast swing music resumes.

JIM:
　　So Lloyd drove to New Mexico
　　But there the story was the same
　　They'd been there, that's for sure
　　But then they'd taken off again
　　It was the same in Texas
　　In Utah and Atlanta
　　Lloyd chased that pair through Arizona
　　Maine and Montana.

SADIE:
　　But no matter how fast he drove
　　He always seemed to be too late
　　They were there the day before
　　But now they're in another state
　　So Lloyd drove pretty steady
　　For near a hundred days
　　Chasin' that big Kenworth
　　Through the entire U.S.A.

*Music stops. This time JIM narrates while SADIE plays the dispatcher,
wearing a huge pair of sunglasses.*

JIM:
  It was in Florida that Lloyd
  Heard the news about his wife
  She'd split up with the Kenworth
  And had taken a brand new life
  She was driving by herself now
  The dispatcher said she earned
  Thirty thousand dollars
  With a big American firm.

Molly appears as the Statue of Liberty, an American apparition, drinking champagne.

  Among truckers she was famous
  And everyone agreed
  Molly was the hottest driver
  In the entire company.

LLOYD is completely crushed.

SADIE: *as DISPATCHER*
  Have a nice day, Lloyd.

LLOYD literally crawls back to his Mack truck. The band plays the whistling campfire theme, very sad.

JIM:
  It was then poor Lloyd realized
  He was a beaten man
  Molly had taken citizenship
  And become an American
  So Lloyd gave up the chase because
  In his heart he knew
  Molly was gone forever
  There was nothing he could do.

LLOYD drives and weeps bitterly.

SADIE:
  So Lloyd drove back to Canada
  A sad and weary man
  He said:

LLOYD:
  If I must live alone
  It will be in my native land.

JIM:
> But Lloyd kept on truckin'
> An independent to the end.

SADIE:
> And that old and rusty Mack truck
> Was his only friend.

LLOYD embraces his truck, then steps forward and speaks to the audience.

LLOYD:
> Now there's a moral to this story
> Though we hope we're not bein' rude
> Everyone has someone who
> Deserves their gratitude
> But there will *always* be a Kenworth
> Ready to take it all away
> And everyone knows that loneliness
> Is a bitter price to pay
> You've got to count your blessings
> Everybody knows it's true
> And the blessings that you squander
> Can be taken away from you.

LLOYD sings a slow verse of "Molly."

> That's the end, and although I'm sad and sorry
> I realize that I'm a wiser man
> I still drive my truck
> And when I'm down on my luck
> I count my blessings, and I do the best I can

> Though my heart is broke I'm wishin' and I'm hopin'
> That she'll think of me with kindness in her heart
> I'm tellin' you, dear Molly
> If you're ever melancholy
> Come up north, we'll make a brand new start.

To tempo, joined by JIM, SADIE, and MOLLY.

> Molly . . .
> Is out there on that highway
> Molly . . .
> Just up and ran away
> Molly . . .

Is somewhere on that highway
Molly . . .
Went and made her getaway.

Epilogue/Finale

On the 401

Chevy wagon, loaded down
Headed out of London town
Four kids and a tent, on vacation
Two throw up before their destination
Daddy's temper is gettin' hot
Mom is wonderin' what they forgot
Kids are bored, one's in tears
Hope it doesn't rain this year
Headed for a trailer park
Tell ghost stories in the dark
Swim and fish, they'll all have fun
Them families . . .
On the 401.

Patrol car crouched just out of sight
Down his leg a yellow stripe
Eyes glued to the radar screen
Fingers stained with nicotine
Catch someone doin' seventy-five
Slam that car into overdirve
Siren is music to his ears

Fill that speeder's heart with fear
Give that driver stern advice
Break the law, you pay the price
With his pointed hat, his badge and gun
The cop is king . . .
On the 401

Travelling salesman, all alone
Got a wife and kids at home
Front seat of a Ford is where he lives
Lonely as a fugitive
Prospective clients on his mind
One eye out for the cops behind
Hands are tense on the steering wheel
As he races on from deal to deal
Every day the same old sell
Every night the same hotel
He'll drink alone when day is done
Friends are scarce . . .
On the 401.

Dodge charger, chopped down low
Cruisin' with nowhere to go
Seventeen, he's got a job
Loves to hear that engine throb
Finance company owns his soul
But in that car he's in control
The car drinks every cent he spends
But he's the envy of his friends
Stereo tape playin' good and loud
Passin' cars and feelin' proud
Drinkin' beer and havin' fun
He's a child . . .
On the 401.

The concrete river, miles and miles
Everyone in single file
Chevrolets and Cadillacs
Limousines all shiny black
I see them all, rich and poor
Pensioners on package tours
Honeymooners on wedding nights
Waving ribbons pink and white

Hondas and Electro-glides
Speeders bent on suicide
All humanity, everyone
Is racing down . . .
The 401.

The song ends. Slow fade to black.

Curtain.

Rock and Roll

Preface

But I was so much older, then
I'm younger than that, now...

—Bob Dylan

The year 1978 didn't start off particularly well for me. I was living in a semi-slum above a barber shop on Bloor Street West in Toronto, barely able to scrape together the monthly rent, when my building became the subject of an ownership dispute. Suddenly I had two landlords, Mr. Demopolus and Mr. MacPhee, each claiming himself to be my true and only landlord and the other a criminal. They would arrive at my door on alternate dates armed with legal-looking documents and, since they were equally shifty and untrustworthy, I paid my rent on a first-come-first-served basis. That was a mistake, because in late January I paid Mr. Demopolus when it was Mr. MacPhee who had control of the heat.

In early February, my suite became very cold. I had a small fireplace, but Bloor Street is no place to be cutting your own firewood, and the grocery store Presto-Log might as well be a hologram for all the heat it emits. I shivered about the place in sweaters and coat, reflecting on the fact that, in Canada, heat makes all the difference. My hitherto cozy, familar little nook became as alien to my life and as indifferent to my needs as outer space. I contracted a bad cold, then the flu. Human life is fragile, easily snuffed out by a turn of the thermostat.

Then suddenly my luck turned. Malcolm Black telephoned to say that he was going on sabbatical from his teaching position at York University, and would I like to replace him for a semester at several hundred dollars per week? I accepted with pathetic eagerness, and a few days later the heat returned. Evidently I had been punished enough. I was able to write again, to complete a first draft of *Billy Bishop Goes to War*. Then with the first rays of spring sunshine came a call from Richard Ouzounian, offering to produce *18 Wheels* at Festival Lennoxville, and to hire me as a director and musician as well.

By late summer, I was a middle-class person, a car-owner, looking forward to *Billy Bishop Goes To War*, which Christopher Wootten had offered to produce at the Vancouver East Cultural Centre.

Things were looking up for me, more than at any time since my birth, so I readily accepted the invitation from Rod Norrie to return to Truro, Nova Scotia, for a reunion concert of my old rock and roll band, The Lincolns. Had the call come a few months earlier I would have refused. I wouldn't have been able to afford the trip home and, besides, nobody likes a reunion when they're down and out.

I arrived in Truro to find my former colleagues in a prefabricated hut full of sound equipment, arguing about which songs to play, looking overweight and tense. The potential for humiliation seemed overwhelming. Rod Norrie had not played drums in ten years, and when we attempted ''Boney Maroney,'' he had to stop briefly in the middle to rest his arms. Apart from our diminished technical skills, there was the sound itself to consider. Sound production had come a long way in ten years thanks to the Japanese, and audiences had come to expect quality. What was an exciting live sound in 1968 could be a laughing-stock ten years later.

We sensed that we could be making fools of ourselves, which was a grim prospect, for the band was an important memory to all of us. There was something about that time that we knew we would never know again, that we didn't want to see desecrated now.

For me the Lincolns represent one of life's local miracles. A group of unexceptional teenaged males, from different classes, religions and parts of town, got together to play music, or something like music, contrary to the wishes of every authority figure in town, and stayed together in various incarnations for seven years, attracting audiences of up to a thousand with no agent and no recording contract. The Lincolns were stars, without in any way becoming involved in the business and the machinery we associate with stardom, a spontaneous eruption in a society that does not ordinarily encourage spontaneity in its citizens.

There was nothing original about the songs we played, which were straight from Philadelphia and Detroit, but we didn't give a hoot about originality. We were like medieval iconographers dispensing sacred images. The Lincolns were the present, local embodiment of a distant holiness. We gave flesh to the Word and shared its authority. We weren't about to question the Word.

Rehearsal technique was simple: we put on a 45 of the song we wanted to learn, then everyone tried to learn their parts, all at once. Of course nobody had the patience to listen to the song from beginning to end before attempting to play it, so within four bars the guitar player was chording to a song he didn't know, soon to be joined in cacophony by everyone else. Gradually we learned the song, mostly by clairvoyance. We flailed away at it for an hour until it began to take some sort of shape, and cleaned up the rough edges in performance. The result was nothing like the original arrangement. Inadvertently, The Lincolns had their own unique sound. Is that creativity? Or were we just a bad copy of someone else?

These thoughts drifted through my head as we practised song after song and opening night approached. What was the meaning of all this? Did it have any significance or was it all just the common antics of dull, derivative sensibilities?

On the positive side, the band's original sound was intact, such as it was. None of us had ever practised much, and not practising is a little like not cleaning your room. If you have the stomach to hold firm, the room will reach its level, after which it will never get any worse, and may well achieve a certain Bohemian cachet.

On Opening Night we were as ready as we were ever going to be, and the evening went far better than expected, in fact it was spectacular. In Truro, they're still talking about it. Two thousand people attended (the number is rising as the incident becomes mythology), some having travelled thousands of miles, and all our worries about the quality of our sound were groundless, for sound perception is as subjective as sexual attraction and, to our audience, we were still the best band around because The Lincolns was *their band*. All my concerns about the band's aesthetics and its cultural significance suddenly seemed vain and banal. What did "originality" have to do with anything, when the music belonged to the audience and the band alike?

We finished the concert with what can only be described as a feeling of lightness, a sense that a perceived weight was the common property of a great many people, that we didn't have to take that part of our lives quite so seriously, that we could relax.

I knew there was a musical there somewhere. Not only was it a good story, it would give me the opportunity to write some rock and roll, which would be a step in the right direction. Up until then I had been writing country and folk tunes, imitation Kurt Weill, turn-of-the-century ballads, war songs and ragtime. It would be like coming home again to write a style of music that I had once actually played.

Later that fall, Eric Peterson and I began performing *Billy Bishop Goes To War*. There began a four-year period during which I didn't worry about landlords because I didn't live anywhere. We occupied a transient netherworld of hotel rooms and sublet apartments, and I'm not certain which accommodation was the more alienating. There was the sterile (not necessarily in the hygienic sense) hotel room with its generic furniture, unlimited edition prints and wrapped toilet seat. Then there was the sublet, warmed by the books and personal paraphernalia of somebody else's life, mute reminders that I had lent (lent? Not after a year or so) all my own effects, that I was now the Phantom Man who slunk through town, invisible outside the theatre, the ghost on tour.

That was my life for four years. Like the truck driver, I moved in the spaces between places, the perfect place from which to write about home, for there are some things you have to be away to understand, important things that are only visible from away. Living in a hotel room in a strange city in 1979 provided me with enough peripheral breathing space to work on *Rock and Roll*, a musical about my home town, and to remember the details, unclouded by the contradictory present.

The title suggested itself very early; the combination of words implied an approach to life; an alternating rigidity and flexibility, both of which seem essential if one is to survive life's inevitable and various transitions. Sometimes you have to be a rock; sometimes you have to roll with it. The trick is know when.

For that you need the advice of Screamin' John McGee, who combines the energy and the idealism of youth with the wisdom of hindsight: a self-contradictory paragon of insight I think you have to be dead to achieve. I derived the name from a local singer named Screamin' Jay Paris, who sang with the Novatones in the late 1950s. I have never seen the man in my life, and know nothing about him.

While I was teaching at York University, one of my duties was to direct a student production of *Our Town*, and there was something about the character of the Stage Manager that I felt a deep desire to parody. In Screamin' John I wanted to create that Stage Manager's nasty Canadian relative, who has similar insights, but without all the pious wisdom, without all the answers. The graveyard scene in Act Two came out of a similar impulse, particularly the litany of the dead and how they died, and Brent's conclusion that, in his words, "There are a lot of people who are dead now, who weren't dead before."

The characters in *Rock and Roll* were originally patterned after people I knew in Truro, but the internal dramatic demands of the piece took over very quickly, and all the characters underwent various metamorphoses, until by the final draft they resembled nobody other than themselves.

I named the town Mushaboom because, in the popular mythology of Nova Scotia, Mushaboom is nowhere, although in reality it is not far from Eecum Seecum. Every region in Canada has a town people refer to as nowhere, whether it is Medicine Hat, Alberta or Wawa, Ontario. It's a way people have of sublimating the feeling that their own town is nowhere, that they themselves are nowhere, that everything important is happening someplace else.

I wrote in a desultory way throughout 1979, and by the time we performed *Billy Bishop* in Ottawa I had several songs and some scenes as well. I played one of the songs for John Wood, who was Artistic Director at the National Arts Centre, and he offered to produce the musical as a vehicle for Frank McKay who, as coincidence would have it, had been the lead singer with The Lincolns and, in part, the model for the character of Parker. Wood had "discovered" McKay in Halifax, had hired him as part of his resident acting company in Ottawa, and I think he felt guilty because he had been unable to give McKay a major role. For whatever peripheral motives, Wood was a great source of support and advice, and I began to write with the National Arts Centre in mind. Before this I had been writing for the usual collection of converted churches, warehouses and funeral parlours that had showcased my work in the past.

To open at the National Arts Centre meant that I was given

technical support and an adequate rehearsal schedule: four weeks of rehearsals, followed by two weeks of previews on tour in Ontario, followed by a week of technicals and previews. For a Broadway musical this would be pathetically inadequate, but it is the most generous I have ever had. *Don Messer's Jubilee*, for example, was rehearsed in under two weeks, previewed twice, then opened for the nation's critics to decide whether or not it was art, whether I was on my way up or down, whether I was a hero or a bum. By contrast, in Europe it is not unusual for a production to be rehearsed for a year.

I am able to survive this kind of pressure, but at a price: when I know I will have only two weeks to prepare the production for public viewing, with no time for experimentation or for rewrites, I write for that reality: structures that can reasonably be achieved under the circumstances allotted. My shows tend to be long on simplicity and short on innovation as a result: minimalist, direct, and cheap.

I don't know whether this is a good thing or a bad thing. In a sense these are formal limitations like the syllables of a Haiku that free me from having to make some difficult choices. Perhaps I would become paralyzed and unfocussed were I given more options. On the other hand, I do know that we continued to work on *Billy Bishop Goes to War* throughout the four years and 500-odd performances we gave, and to this day I believe that our last performance was our best. In the case of *Rock and Roll*, I don't think it would have been produced at all if it weren't for the National Arts Centre: I would have been in the hospital.

The logistical problems of combining drama with rock and roll in a situation where the actors play their own instruments were truly nightmarish. To begin with, the actors had to make a credible rock and roll band, to trace the group's progress from incompetent beginners to seasoned, slightly jaded veterans. And rock and roll involves tons of musical equipment that must be brought out and stowed, donned and shed, several times in an evening. On top on that were the usual problems making a show work dramatically when one can never be certain whether a problem is onstage or with the script itself, a script that has never been proven to work, and perhaps never will. It can make you insecure, when you're responsible for everything.

The first previews were rocky. I burst into tears in the lobby after the first Kingston performance. Desperate, I called Eric Peterson in Saskatchewan to come quick. Peterson is someone whose agreement I can trust: if we agree it will work, it will work. If we don't agree, it won't work. The issue then is agreement, not who is right. With Peterson I might emerge from the Tower of Babel I was in. A director/writer/composer is never short of advice from people who will suffer no damage if they are wrong, and they all have the same toe in your ribs: "But John, you're too close to it all! You don't have the perspective!"

Peterson arrived, and the weather began to clear. At least the casting was working out: the actors were all very good and, more than that, were more interested in the show than in the progress of their own careers. This isn't always the case, and a show can disintegrate into a humiliating every-man-for-himself rout. But *Rock and Roll* enjoyed a solidarity associated with London during the Blitz, with . . . well, with rock and roll bands on tour. And in Cochrane we received our first standing ovation. Things were looking up. It might work, after all.

The interviews for *Rock and Roll* were more debilitating than usual. The first question was always the same: "Why write *Rock and Roll*, when *Grease* has already been done?", the assumption being that a U.S. musical about the Fifties should be more than enough to cover Canada in the early Sixties, that there was really nothing more to be said. Then the next question was: "Will this be as successful as *Billy Bishop*? Are you going to Broadway again? Are you on your way up, or are you on your way down?" This can get you down. It can make you wonder where you are, where the people around you think *they* are.

In the end, everything turned out as well as could be hoped. *Rock and Roll* opened on March 16, 1981 at the National Arts Centre to favourable notices and generous audiences, toured British Columbia, then ran for eleven weeks at the Vancouver East Cultural Centre as part of a co-production agreement with the National Arts Centre. A revised version toured Canada in 1983, again produced by the Vancouver East Cultural Centre.

In 1984 I co-directed a feature-length video based on the piece, entitled *The King of Friday Night*. We shot the feature in Truro, Nova Scotia, and the dance sequences took place in the Legion Hall where *The Lincolns* had played for five years. Many of the extras were people who had attended our dances then. Shirly Hamilton of the Colchester Players cast some of the smaller parts, and played a cameo, as did my 100-year-old grandmother. It was eerie to be re-living the whole thing at age thirty-eight in such detail, to be sleeping in my old bed every night, with my parents sleeping down the hall: it involved a converging of past and present, a scrambling of time and place, prompting the suspicion that perhaps life isn't just a march to the cliff and over. Maybe it's a little more complicated than that.

I haven't discussed this with the other Lincolns. They aren't the introspective type.

Rock and Roll was originally produced by the National Arts Centre, in co-production with the Vancouver East Cultural Centre, and starred Frank McKay, Page Fletcher, Barbara Williams, Alec Willows, Andy Rhodes and John C. Rutter. Sets and costumes were designed by Arthur Penson, and lights by Nick Cernovitch. The Musical Director was J. Douglas Dodd, who also played piano accompaniment with Ed Henderson on guitar. The production was stage managed by Paul Shaw, and directed by John Gray.

The King of Friday Night was co-produced by Canamedia and the Canadian Broadcasting Corporation.

The playwright/composer would like to acknowledge the contributions and encouragement of Eric Peterson, Beverlee Larsen, John Wood and The Lincolns.

Rock and Roll

Characters

CHINK, an unemployed underachiever, misanthropic and dissatisfied with his lot in life.

MANNY, the rich kid. Inherited wealth is his cross.

BRENT, a working-class overachiever catapulted into the lower middle class, an insurance adjuster who suspects that he may have missed something.

SHIRLY, wife to BRENT and the Monarchs' biggest fan, despite everything.

SCREAMIN' JOHN McGEE, the Ghost of Rock and Roll.

PARKER, the fat kid who sings.

Place

A small Canadian town called Mushaboom.

Time

1980, 1960 and 1965.

Songs

"In the Time of Our Lives"	The Monarchs
"Just a Memory"	Parker & Shirly
"Never Did Nothin'"	Parker & Shirly
"You're Gonna Be a Star"	Chink, Manny & Brent
"Let Me Walk You Home"	Chink, Manny & Brent
"Play a Little Rock and Roll"	Screamin' John
"I'll Beat the Shit Out of Him"	Chink, Manny & Brent
"The Boys' Club"	Shirly
"This Could Be the Night"	Screamin' John
"The Fat Boy"	Parker
"Moncton Medley"	The Monarchs

Act One

Silhouetted on the darkened stage amid their instruments and amplifiers, the Monarchs sing "In the Time of Our Lives," a capella. It is 1980, and they are standing on the stage of the Mushaboom Legion Hall. There is a portrait of Queen Elizabeth II over the proscenium arch.

In the time of our lives
Our footsteps were sure
Ideals were intact
And our motives were pure
No failures to mourn
Or regrets to endure
We were having the time of our lives.

We remember the kicks
Thanks to memory's tricks
And it all seems so vivid and clear.

So let's raise a glass
To all those who survived
What was surely the time of our lives
We were having the time of our lives.

Lights up. MANNY, BRENT, CHINK, and PARKER are raising bottles of Alexander Keith's ale in a toast.

The four men are variously dressed, according to their stations in life: MANNY is in an expensive suit and wears a heavy gold watch; BRENT is in a plaid polyester sports jacket and clip-on tie; CHINK wears a plaid jacket, soiled work pants and Kodiak boots; PARKER is wearing a suit, cowboy boots, and an open-neck shirt with a gold chain around his neck.

They savour the last chord of "In the Time of Our Lives."

MANNY: God, that's beautiful. Boys, if you would lift your bottles with me, I'd like to propose a little toast.

MANNY, BRENT & PARKER: Hear, hear! Hear, hear!

MANNY, BRENT and PARKER hum "In the Time of Our Lives" as MANNY speaks.

MANNY: On behalf of the Sports Association, I'd like to thank you boys for comin' out, and welcome you to the First Monarchs Reunion.

CHINK: Stupid idea if you ask me.

They stop humming.

MANNY: Shut up. I put up enough with you fifteen years ago.

CHINK: We're too friggin' old.

MANNY: Shut up!

BRENT: Chink, don't be negative. Manny, pay no attention.

MANNY: Thank you, Brent. First I'd like to thank Parker here for interrupting a successful show business career . . .

CHINK: "Tie a Yellow Ribbon" on the "Chuck Queasy Show" ain't exactly a high point if you ask me . . .

MANNY: Will you please shut up? You're givin' me a colitis attack.

PARKER: Yeah, lay off, Chink.

CHINK: *to PARKER* If we look like assholes it could take the gloss off your triumphant return.

PARKER: Thanks a lot, Chink.

MANNY: *to CHINK* You're spoilin' everything!

BRENT: Pay no attention, guys. You know what he's like.

CHINK: This is stupid. I'm gonna have to go incognito in my own home town!

MANNY: *losing control* I'm gonna have to kill him. I'm just gonna . . .

PARKER: This is all very familiar.

BRENT: *to CHINK* Can you please keep a civil tongue in your head just this once?

CHINK: Fifteen hundred tickets sold. What's happenin' to the money, Manny?

MANNY: You Judas asshole, if I didn't need you I'd shoot you! The money's goin' to the Sports Association so a bunch of poor kids can play ball!

CHINK: Jeez, you're generous with other people's time and money! The De Medici of Colchester County!

MANNY: What the hell did you call me!?

MANNY makes a move toward CHINK. BRENT steps between them. It's an old reflex. There is a sullen pause. Enter SHIRLY, an attractive woman in her thirties, dressed in jeans and an old shirt of BRENT's.

SHIRLY: Well how's the reunion goin'?

BRENT helps SHIRLY onto the stage. They kiss out of habit.

BRENT: Terrible, dear. Just terrible.

SHIRLY: I knew this was going to happen. I knew it would be too much to expect you guys to have a kind word to say to each other.

BRENT: This band is very important to a lot of people's memories. We're history, like the Mayflower, the Plains of Abraham . . .

SHIRLY: And they don't remember you as a bunch of creeps.

BRENT: They're gonna want to hear us just like in the old days, and I am worried sick!

CHINK: I borrowed Bobby Carruthers' bass, but I been too scared to try and play it.

MANNY: Yeah, well I haven't had a decent shit in a month and a half.

CHINK: Maybe it's all that money stuck up your ass.

MANNY goes for CHINK, who jumps off the stage to escape. BRENT moves quickly to get between them.

MANNY: I'm gonna have to kill him! I'm just gonna . . .

BRENT: All right, now hold it!

SHIRLY: You guys make me sick, you know that?

Pause. MANNY calms down.

PARKER: OK boys, come on, now! Manny, what about that nice toast you were proposin'? Let's get off to a good start.

CHINK, BRENT, PARKER and SHIRLY hum "In the Time of Our Lives" under MANNY's toast.

MANNY: Boys, you don't know what this means to me! She's been fifteen years, boys, fifteen long and rewarding years. But deep in my heart I know that in all those years I never had as much fun as I had with the Monarchs. And I just gotta say that I never had one friend like I had friends with the Monarchs. Those were the best years of my life, and they'll never come back! Not ever! You think I care about the Sports Association? Piss on the Sports Association! Just give me a taste of it, boys! Just a taste is all I want!
CHINK: Fuck off, Manny. You know what it was really like.

Music: the introduction to "Never Did Nothin'." Two spotlights hit PARKER and SHIRLY, who sing:

We had trouble with Mom
We had trouble with Dad
We had a face full of zits
It was the worst we ever had
Shavin' the hair from above our lips
Starin' at the girls who were growin' tits.

That's what we did when we were kids
Shootin' the shit on garbage lids
Never saw nothin'
Never said nothin'
We never did nothin' at all.

We had beady eyes
We had runny beaks
When we tried to talk
It would come out in squeaks
Stuffin' Ban into smelly pits
Starin' at the girls who were growin' tits.

That's what we did we sure were sad
We talked so big and we looked so bad
Never saw nothin'
Never said nothin'
We never did nothin' at all.

Ooo-wah-ooo
Never saw nothin', never said nothin'
Ooo-wah-ooo
We never did nothin' at all.

Goin' to school
Like we're in a trance
Hidin' the bulges
In our pants
Holdin' pencils chewed to bits
Starin' at the girls who were growin' tits.

That's what we did when we were young
The one excitement was the song we sung
Never saw nothin'
Never said nothin'
We never did nothin' at all.

Ooo-wah-ooo
Never saw nothin', never said nothin'
Ooo-wah-ooo
We never did nothin' at all.

The song's hard rock ending goes immediately to a single piano intro-duction to "Just a Memory," which is sung by PARKER and SHIRLY:

Don't you know it's just a memory
Got no particular reality
Oh, a foggy memory
It was so long ago.

A simple memory
Not a thing to do with you or me
Think of it as just a fantasy
It was so long ago
So long ago.

The piano continues, and a spotlight hits CHINK, who is yawning and scratching his arm. CHINK addresses the audience.

CHINK: Did you notice what I was doin' there? I was yawning and scratching my arm. Here in Mushaboom we do a lot of that. Yawn-ing and scratching the old arm. We like it. It passes the time. Why Jeez, there's twenty-three guys standin' in front of George's right now, and I swear to God every last one of them is yawning and scratching his arm. For hours and hours. So when Manny and me got the idea we were gonna start a band, the event kind of stands out in the social landscape of Mushaboom, like a tree in a vacant lot. You see, ideas ain't a common thing in Mushaboom. And culture? That's somethin' you find in the back of your fridge every couple of months. Maybe we wanted to be the toast of Mushaboom. Maybe we wanted to be like Screamin' John McGee, who was nineteen and played the school dances. Maybe we wanted to get some tail for once in our lives. All I know is it was the closest I ever came to being employed.

The piano accompaniment continues. In another part of the stage, a spotlight hits BRENT and SHIRLY, who address the audience.

BRENT: This is a very special week for Shirly and myself, because this is the week we burn the mortgage.

SHIRLY: One thirty-six Cross Avenue. There's a little sign on the lawn that says, "Brent and Shirly."

BRENT: Cross Avenue is on the west side. My family came from Elmdale Road: that's on the east side.

SHIRLY: My family lives just around the corner. In fact, you could say I've lived on the same block all my life. But we do subscribe to the *National Geographic*.

BRENT: As soon as I could crawl I started working my way from the east side of Mushaboom to the west side of Mushaboom.

SHIRLY: Aren't those little wooden ducks cute? Brent made them in his workshop.

BRENT: I was a mature child. I had a paper route, I shovelled snow, I collected pop bottles. Other kids had colouring books: I had a ledger.

SHIRLY: I was always musical. I knew every song that ever made the Top Ten. I knew the colour preferences of every singer on "Music Hop." I love music more than anything.

BRENT: I had a bad reversal when I was twelve. I caught Osgood Slater's Disease and had to spend six months with casts on my legs. Dad brought home an old guitar, so I strung it up and played along with the radio. Busy hands are happy hands.

SHIRLY: If I'd have been a boy I'd have played with a rock and roll band but, since I was a girl, I went out with the guitar player. It was the natural thing to do.

BRENT: Then Chink asked me to join the band. Well, Osgood Slater left me months behind financially, so I did. The decision was not frivolous.

SHIRLY: Brent and I fell in love and got married.

102

The piano accompaniment continues. On another part of the stage, a spotlight hits MANNY, who is holding a photograph so that the audience can see it.

MANNY: This is a picture of my mom and dad. If you look closely you can see they're standing in front of the Presbyterian Church. That's because my family practically owns the Presbyterian Church. See that stained glass? That's ours. The fresh paint? That's ours too. We're very well thought of in the Presbyterian Church, and that's quite an achievement because my grandparents were Jewish. D.B.—that's my dad—D.B. owns the Buy-Rite Department Store, a paper mill, four apartment buildings in Halifax and ten per cent of Cape Breton. He says it's because he's a Christian now. Jesus has done a lot for D.B. because D.B. has done a lot for Jesus. I remember when I was very small I asked him what God was. D.B. told me: "God is the President of a very large holding company, and you've got to suck up to Him if you want to get ahead." D.B. never approved of the Monarchs. He said we were following Satan, we'd be poor. But I liked playing the drums because it gave me the chance to hit something really hard, and pretend it was D.B.

The piano accompaniment continues. Spot on PARKER.

PARKER: I live in Toronto now because of the opportunity. My agent says I'm gonna be the Wayne Newton of the North. But when they asked me to join the Monarchs it was the first time anybody had ever asked me to join anything. I really like these guys.

PARKER and SHIRLY sing a conclusion to "Just a Memory":

This is the story of a band you know
(Don't you know)
A band that might have slipped your mind, although
(So long ago)
You grew up with it long ago
It was so long ago.

Don't you know it's just a memory
Got no particular reality
Think of it as just a fantasy
It was so long ago
(So long ago)
It was so long ago

(So long ago)
It was so long ago
(So long ago).

Blackout. A spot appears front stage centre. CHINK delivers a monologue while the other characters change costume.

CHINK: By now you got the idea that this thing didn't happen in Singapore, Tahiti or Paris. Nope, you're in Mushaboom and there's some difference. You're standin' at the corner of Provost and Commercial and you got a bunch of stores: shoe stores, jewellery stores, and clothing stores like Preston Tupper. Everybody comes out of Preston Tupper lookin' like Perry Como. Don't matter who you are, you're gonna look like Perry Como when you get out of there. I've seen guys go in, buy a black leather jacket, black chino pants, Cuban heel boots, and still come out lookin' exactly like Perry Como. At the end of the street is D.B.'s department store. My mom's been workin' for D.B. since 1945, and I can tell you from experience that Unemployment Insurance pays a lot better. Around the corner is Spencer's Pool Hall. According to our school principal, every guy that ever shot a game there is now in jail. Crime is a disease you catch off the felt in Spencer's Pool Hall. It's a pretty normal small town in its opinions: the coloured people are lazy, the Jews are a bunch of stingy cheats, the Arabs are vicious and the Chinese feed you cat meat in your chop suey. A real humanitarian town. You know the kind I mean. As a matter of fact, even bein' white won't let you off the hook. You're basically in trouble if you don't look like . . . Perry Como. Forget it if you're too fat or too skinny or too anything else. Mind you, Mushaboom ain't all that bad. A lot of people when they go out and see the world come tearin' back to Mushaboom because in comparison it looks real good.

CHINK takes off his jacket and throws it aside. He puts up his shirt collar. He combs his hair into a ducktail and puts on sunglasses.

But when you're sixteen, and you're stuck here, you're just prayin' on bended knee to get the hell out!

We hear the sound of a guitar, being played very badly. Lights up to reveal BRENT, in chinos and a sports cardigan, circa 1960. CHINK joins him onstage and together they sing "You're Gonna Be a Star." It sounds just terrible.

Gonna play some rock and roll
Just for kicks
Household Finance will lend
The money real quick
Get yourself a booking in the Legion hall
Everybody's gonna have a ball.

You're gonna be a star
You play your cheap guitar
Soon you'll buy a car
Oh baby, you'll go far
You're gonna be a star.

The song breaks down. BRENT and CHINK stop playing, depressed.

BRENT: Boy oh boy, that's awful. I mean, gee whiz!

CHINK: I never heard anything like it. Shitstick!

BRENT: I wonder if Simpson's will give us a refund on this stuff. Gosh, we're in trouble already!

CHINK: Drums! You can't play rock and roll without drums! Where is that son of a whore?

BRENT: Well how should I know?

MANNY enters, dejected. He is wearing expensive 1960s clothing but with no sense of style. He is carrying a battered cymbal that falls to the floor with a clatter.

CHINK: About time you got here, Man! Where are the drums?

MANNY: D.B. took them and locked them away in the cellar.

BRENT: Well what in the heck did he do that for?

MANNY: Locked them away in the cellar, said they belonged under the earth next to hell along with Satan, Judas and Krushchev. I had to borrow some.

CHINK: Where the hell are they, then?

MANNY: Right out here.

He exits and immediately returns with a huge military snare drum, the kind you strap around your shoulder. He gives it a couple of tentative taps.

CHINK: What have we here?

MANNY: The drums. I borrowed them off of fat Donny Parker. His dad plays with the Mushaboom Symphonic Band.

BRENT is in a panic.

CHINK: Nice.

BRENT: *to MANNY* So that's it? My life savings down the toilet and you show up with that? I paid two hundred bucks for this stuff! Do you have any idea how many pop bottles that is?

CHINK: Well what about me? My reputation isn't worth a pinch of shit! I tell Walker Douglas a hundred lies and get the Debert Legion! Now everybody in Colchester County's gonna hear two songs, two guitars and no drums! A real musical evening!

MANNY: Will you guys stop picking on me? C'mon! It's not my fault! D.B.'s probably got my drums burnt by now! Mom's just going to have to send for a new set.

This infuriates CHINK, whose bass represents a great sacrifice on the part of his mother.

CHINK: You pointy headed asshole! You told me you had a set of drums! Your mother buys you everything short of a Boeing Interceptor! Maybe if you're a good boy she'll buy you a fuckin' brain!

MANNY, who has great physical courage, goes for CHINK. CHINK, who has not, runs. BRENT intervenes.

MANNY: You scum-sucking bat! You rat's prick!

CHINK: Keep him off me, Brent! Keep him off me!

MANNY: Let me go, Brent! His ribs are comin' right out!

BRENT: Come on now, you guys, stop it! We gotta play the dance! We just gotta! We gotta play the darned thing or we might as well blow our brains out.

They think about this.

CHINK: We're gonna be humiliated.

BRENT: We can make a success of this if we really try.

MANNY: Yeah, well D.B. says if God had meant for us to play rock and roll, He would have made us a different colour.

CHINK: We're gonna make people wish they were deaf.

They have been putting on their instruments. Now they are ready.

BRENT: Come on, you guys! This isn't just music, you know! This is money!

Lights immediately change so that the stage is now in a dance hall at night. There is a mirror ball. CHINK steps up to the mike and acts as lead singer and emcee. They play a shattering chord, as though they have just finished a song, a chord that also serves to punctuate the end of the previous scene.

On tape, we hear the sound of an unfriendly audience who are becoming more and more hostile.

AUDIENCE: Boo! Hiss! Boo!

CHINK: Thank you! That was Johnny B. Goode!

AUDIENCE MEMBER #1: We know! We know!

AUDIENCE MEMBER #2: That's the tenth time you played that one!

CHINK: Whew! Whew! Hoo boy, we're really havin' a ball tonight!

AUDIENCE MEMBER #3: Oh no, we're not!

AUDIENCE MEMBER #2: We want our money back! Kill the band!

Boos and hisses.

CHINK: This will be your home waltz! *to* BRENT *and* MANNY Let's get this thing going before they come for us.

They play an excruciating home waltz, "Let Me Walk You Home":

Oh my love is true
Just for you
Oh please, please love me too
Don't leave me all alone
Let me walk you home.

You're just sixteen
A teenage queen
You're the prettiest chick I ever seen
Don't leave me all alone . . .
Let me walk you home.

Got a white sport coat
Brylcreem in my hair
Got some pointed shoes
And some time to spare
But all that style
Just don't mean a thing
If you won't
Won't wear my ring . . .

I'll hold your hand
I'll treat you right
I'll meet your dad

I'll be polite
Don't leave me all alone . . .
Let me walk you home.

The song ends, to taped boos and hisses.

CHINK: Thank you! Thank you!
AUDIENCE MEMBERS: What a shitty dance! You bastards! You guys are *sick!*

The taped voices fade.

CHINK: Whew! Whew! We really had a ball tonight!

The lights come up full, and any romance is gone, to be replaced by stark reality. The band members put down their instruments, depressed. MANNY throws his battered cymbal to the floor with a clatter. Pause.

CHINK: I think that was the worst night of my life. Well, put it this way: I hope I never have a night that makes this one look good.
MANNY: I thought I was in hell, just like D.B. said.
BRENT: We gotta work on it. We gotta bear down.
MANNY: Brent's right. We can't expect it to sound good right away.
CHINK: Good?? Sound *good??* We got a ways to go to get to mediocre! It's all around town that we made fools of ourselves tonight! This is bad! The comeback's uphill!
MANNY: Well, if we'd thought of a decent name for this band, we could have pretended we were from out of town.
CHINK: What do you want us to do, Manny, wear false noses? Nice, Manny, real nice, you simple . . .

CHINK stops. He has seen something, by the side of the stage. It is SHIRLY, who is trying to get up the courage to speak.

SHIRLY: Hi.
BRENT: Hi.

BRENT is struck by an unfamiliar sensation that has something to do with the newcomer.

SHIRLY: I heard you guys tonight, and I think you need a singer.
CHINK: God give me strength.
SHIRLY: I can sing. I know a lot more songs than you do.
CHINK: Girl, if you're not out of here real quick, I'm gonna forget that I'm a gentleman.
MANNY: Yeah, girl.

SHIRLY: You guys are a bunch of creeps. You sound like creeps too.
CHINK: Why you little . . .

CHINK goes for her with a coward's confidence. BRENT intervenes.
CHINK immediately backs down. BRENT turns to SHIRLY.

BRENT: Ah, sorry, but this is kind of a sensitive band meeting.
Maybe you could come back some other time.
SHIRLY: OK.

Pause. Their eyes meet. BRENT is pole-axed.

BRENT: What's your name, anyway?
SHIRLY: Shirly.
BRENT: I'm Brent.

They shake hands and giggle. MANNY and CHINK look on with
disapproval.

SHIRLY: I've never met a professional musician before.
BRENT: Oh. That's nice.
SHIRLY: Yeah.
BRENT: Well, see you.
SHIRLY: 'Bye.
BRENT: 'Bye.

SHIRLY exits. BRENT watches her until she is out of sight.

CHINK: If there's anything I can't stand it's a smart girl.

MANNY starts to exit.

MANNY: I'm gonna punch some faces and restore some of my
prestige.
BRENT: Wait a second, Manny. There's something we gotta do.
Guys, we're gonna have to talk to Screamin' John.

Pause. This is a very serious step. MANNY and CHINK are alarmed.

CHINK: Screamin' John? What do we wanna talk to Screamin' John
for?
MANNY: You know how old that guy is? Nineteen!
CHINK: He'll laugh in our faces! Tonight is one thing, but it's
another thing to make a fool of yourself in front of Screamin' John!
BRENT: It's the only way. He's played in bands: the Atomics. The
Lincolns. He's been around. We need an experienced ear. We need
new equipment. We need a new name. And I think we gotta learn
to play better.

MANNY: Yeah, but Screamin' John! He's crazy. *giggles* You know what they say about him, eh?

CHINK & BRENT: No. What?

MANNY: Can't let him anywhere near a cat.

CHINK & BRENT: Why?

MANNY: Tear the legs right off it.

CHINK & BRENT: You're kidding! Tear the legs . . .

MANNY, BRENT & CHINK: Right off it!!!

They collapse, laughing. Fast fade to black. We hear a slow blues, featuring a piano and a wailing alto saxophone. A single spot hits SCREAMIN' JOHN McGEE. Greasy, seedy and potentially violent, he is not the kind of role model parents would wish for their teenage sons. He is wearing a tattered, not-too-clean 1950s band uniform and skin-tight pants with pointed Cuban-heeled boots and an extravagant, very greasy ducktail. He is worn and prematurely aged. For the younger boys, he is a man of awesome charisma.

SCREAMIN' JOHN speaks to music, in the manner of 1950s beat poetry but with a feverish energy.

SCREAMIN' JOHN:
  I'm gettin' old, boys: I can sense it
  I don't expect you to know what that feels like, boys, but I'm
    tellin' you the signs are clear
  It all comes to you one morning without word without warning
  You brush your teeth and you comb your hair
  Put on your clothes have a bowl of Cheerios
  And you go into the street to see who you'll meet
  You see the people goin' to and fro to the store or the office
    or the
  Fashion show
  And you say to yourself . . .
  What am I gonna do, today?

We and he hear a high-pitched wail on the alto sax, strange and a bit ominous, followed by silence.

  Suddenly you realize, boys
  That's the first time you asked that question.

The piano blues resumes, rhythmic and sure-footed.

You'd go out, be cool, play some pool
Cruise around town up and down
Hop down to Ernie's garage shoot the shit
With the boys fixin' their continental kits
Smoke some cigarettes drink some beer
Do a little bowlin' then cruise off outta here for some burgers
Maybe try and pick up a chick
Then a little visit to the bootleggers
And you sit around with the lemon gin and you
Shoot the shit with whoever comes in don't matter who don't
   make no difference to you . . .
Used to be what I'd call a full life, boys.

Silence.

But now you don't wanna do none of those things no more
What am I gonna do? What am I gonna do?
Who's gonna give me direction?
You?
You never asked yourself that question before
You just did it, nothin' more.

The piano music resumes. Now it is very eerie.

Visions of mortality
Creep over the floor through the window under the door
You search your body for lumps
Don't laugh, boys, don't make light of lumps
No laughin' and jokin'
You try and stop smokin'
You don't wanna drink with the boys all night
You don't wanna screw you don't wanna fight
And then it comes, one last thought to amaze:
You ain't gonna play in the band no more
You can't take
The days.

*The piano and alto sax play a rhythmic blues, more up-tempo than ever
before, almost a boogie.*

You're all through, boys!
Time to quit the band
Apply for that Assistant Manager's job at Woolworth's
Get married, get that house on the lane
Trade in the Merc for a Chevy Biscayne

Take that promotion, boys!
New house new car new rings in the tub
Maybe maybe maybe join the Kiwanis Club
Then the kids grow up and they leave home
And you find yourself playin' golf
Alone
And time goes by, without a doubt
And your teeth cave in, and your hair falls out
And sooner or later you find that lump
Or that pitter-pat in your chest goes
Thump.

Silence, then a banshee wail from the saxophone.

Death, boys
A dead-end street
I can see my whole life in front of my feet
The star goes out without havin' seen
And it's all over

puzzled:

When you're nineteen?

Let's do a little number to give you a start
Put some rock and roll into your heart
But when you're on your feet we go separate ways
Screamin' John can't take the days.
Gimme an ''E,'' boys.

SCREAMIN' JOHN sings "Play a Little Rock and Roll," an up-tempo rockabilly song. MANNY, BRENT & CHINK back him up with doo-wop harmony and 1950s pop choreography:

Have you got a lot of urges in your body
That you can't control
Get yourself in motion, and
Play a little rock and roll.

Has your heart been hocked
Have your memories all been stole
Get yourself in motion, and
Play a little rock and roll.

Well your hands are shakin'
Your guts are achin'

You can't stop cryin', 'cause
Your heart's just breakin'
Your mind is bitchin'
Your insides are itchin'
While your daddy's in the office
And your momma's in the kitchen.

Gotta do somethin' to soothe
Your doggone soul
Get yourself in motion, and
Play a little rock and roll.

The song goes into a drum and guitar vamp, as SCREAMIN' JOHN speaks, sotto and sinister at first, then growing in intensity and volume:

Rock on, rock on, while you can
You're the soul of a generation, man
Button-down collars and button-down lips
Crew-cut heads and skinny hips
Elvis and Dion, much too scary
Listen to Peter, Paul and Mary
School is just a railway station
All on board for the corporation
Do one thing that's straight and true
Do one thing that you wanted to do
Rock on, rock on, while you can
You're the soul of a generation, man!

SCREAMIN' JOHN screams, then sings a finale:

Boys and girls
Be young before you're old
Get yourself in motion, and
Play a little rock and roll.

Get yourself in motion, and
Play a little rock and roll.

Get yourself in motion, and
Play a little rock and roll.

End song. Blackout.

Spot on CHINK, who is holding his bass guitar, ready to play.

CHINK: Well Jeez, I told you he was crazy. Took us cruisin' in his '53 Monarch, when all the beer was gone the son of a bitch drank a bottle of ink. Next day he lent us some gear from the Blue Cats, showed us how to play "Slippin' and Slidin'" and named us the Monarchs. You might say Screamin' John was like a father to us.

A spotlight hits MANNY, kneeling or standing beside a new set of drums in an attitude of prayer.

MANNY: Dear Lord. M. Bridgeman here. Son of D.B. and Margaret Bridgeman, heir to the Bridgeman fortune. I wish to confess the sins of the band, Lord, for the Monarchs' sins are my sins. In Shubenacadie, Chink and I did push the piano off the stage, just missed two skinny chicks in beehive hairdos and left a big hole in the hardwood floor, this is true. In Bass River Chink did cause a short circuit by pissing on the stage, I did approve. These and all my sins I confess to You, Lord, no problem, but please, please don't let D.B. find out. D.B. is nastier than Thou. Especially don't let D.B. find out about the riot in Pictou when Lonnie Martin got stabbed and Brent and me ended up in jail. That's the time Chink tried to break us out with the lawn mower and we had to bribe the sheriff to keep it out of court. Keep this out of D.B.'s sight and I will not be disinherited, and I will give even more to the Presbyterian Church. I'll even contribute to the Missionary Fund, for I have nothing against savages. These things I ask in Jesus name, Amen.

We hear a screaming guitar introduction to "I'll Beat the Shit Out of Him," played by BRENT, joined on drums and bass by MANNY and CHINK. The band has improved noticeably, but, more than that, radiate confidence and energy. CHINK sings, badly:

Somebody stole my baby
You know the girl that drives me crazy
Beat the shit out of him
I'll beat the shit out of him
I'll beat the shit out of him
You know his name is Jim
I'll beat the shit out of him.
He felt my baby's leg in class
I'll put my big foot up his ass
I'll beat the shit out of him

I'll beat the shit out of him
I'll beat the shit out of him
You know his name is Jim
I'll beat the shit out of him.

BRENT stops playing and brings the song to a halt with difficulty.

BRENT: Hold it! Hold it! *They stop.* There's something we gotta discuss.

MANNY & CHINK: What?

BRENT: I think the band is going astray.

CHINK: You wanna elaborate?

BRENT: Sure. We're turning into a bunch of animals. In six months the name of the Monarchs has gone right down the toilet. Shirly says . . .

MANNY & BRENT: *mimicking contemptuously* Shirly says.

BRENT: *dogged* Shirly says there are parents who won't let their kids come to our dances because they come home drunked-up, beat-up, knocked-up or all three! It's gross.

CHINK: That ain't gross. That's showmanship.

MANNY: No, Brent's right. We've gone too far. I wake up Sunday mornings, I feel ashamed. I feel soiled. Soiled!

SHIRLY enters with a bag of hamburgers from the A&W.

SHIRLY: Feeding time at the zoo.

CHINK: *to SHIRLY* Will you cut that out?

BRENT: As I was saying, Chink, you can only smash so many pianos and pee on so many stages. The novelty wears off.

SHIRLY: So does your welcome.

CHINK: *to SHIRLY* You cut that out. I'm not tellin' you again.

BRENT: We gotta get more musical. We need a singer with . . . talent.

BRENT and MANNY are broaching a sensitive topic.

MANNY: Yeah, Chink. Everybody thinks you're cool, but you can't sing worth a shit.

CHINK is stung.

CHINK: Come on, you guys! I give this band everything I got! Are you callin' me a failure at the first thing I ever tried to do?

Pause.

BRENT: You hit the nail right on the head there, Chink. There's no easy way to tell you, but it's true.

CHINK: Well I'll be buggered.

MANNY: Don't take it too hard, Chink. Everybody's got some sort of talent. Almost everybody.

CHINK: You got talent?

MANNY: I don't need talent. I got money.

CHINK: *nearly in tears* Aw, shit.

BRENT and MANNY pat CHINK on the back in a comforting manner.

SHIRLY: Listen you guys, I can sing.

MANNY is appalled. BRENT is embarrassed.

MANNY: Arrrrrrrgh!

SHIRLY: Well, I really can!

MANNY: Arrrrrrrgh! Brent!

BRENT is torn.

SHIRLY: All you have to do is try me! What have you got to lose?

CHINK turns to BRENT, hurt and angry.

CHINK: I'm willin' to take a lot of humiliation in life, but I will not be replaced by a girl!

BRENT: *embarrassed* Easy there, fella. Calm down.

MANNY: *to SHIRLY* Can't you see what this man's goin' through? You're in pretty poor taste, girl!

SHIRLY: Oh, come on!

BRENT tries to be reasonable.

BRENT: Stop it, Shirly. Girls don't play rock and roll.

SHIRLY: Who says?

MANNY: The Lord says, that's who says.

SHIRLY: *furious* You guys really are a bunch of creeps, you know that? What does it feel like to be that stupid? Do you have little spots on your brain that are numb? Can you feel your lips moving when you read the comics?

MANNY: *stung* What was that?

SHIRLY throws the bag of hamburgers at Brent.

SHIRLY: Here are your hamburgers! You can stuff your face or you can stick them up your bum! I know how hard it is to tell the difference!

The band is shocked. The lights change to isolate SHIRLY. SHIRLY sings "The Boys' Club." Lyrical:

I always had a high opinion
Of myself, when I was small
Yes, I know it's true
But to discover that the world
Just won't agree with me at all
What's a girl to do?

"The Boys' Club" becomes a hard rock number:

Everything is manly
With Tom and Jim and Stanley
At the Boys' Club.

Jim and John and Gerry
Are big and strong and hairy
At the Boys' Club.

The boys are feelin' frisky
Drinkin' beer and whiskey
At the Boys' Club.

Everybody is a joker
They're playin' stud poker
At the Boys' Club.

Cruel is a virtue
Gentle is a sin
No matter how they hurt you
Got to play to win
As long as you're a girl
They'll never let you in
At the Boys' Club.

Big and strong and proud
(Talkin' 'bout the Boys' Club)
This very manly crowd
(Talkin' 'bout the Boys' Club)
Hey, ladies ain't allowed
(She's talkin' 'bout the boys.)

No girl is a match for
All the happy bachelors
At the Boys' Club.

Bernie, Paul and Peter
Get together and defeat her
At the Boys' Club.

Don't tell me that it's nature
I know that's a lie
There's nothing natural 'bout
A bunch of greedy guys
When they tell me that I'm pretty
I'll tell them damn your eyes
Damn the Boys' Club.

(At the Boys' Club)
I'll tell you once again
(At the Boys' Club)
No it's never gonna end
(At the Boys' Club)
Will the boys turn into men
(At the Boys' Club)
Girl you haven't got a friend
At the Boys' Club.

End song. Blackout.

*On piano we hear the introduction to a waltz, "This Could Be the Night."
Lights up. In the background we see a night sky, full of stars and a cres-
cent moon, and the outline of pine trees. We see the lit tail lights of a
1959 Chevrolet, or rather the significant components of a 1959 Chevrolet:
the tail lights and fins. BRENT carefully backs into position onstage.
SHIRLY is in the passenger seat. BRENT turns off the engine and the
tail lights go out. Silence. We hear the sound of crickets.*

BRENT: I guess we might as well turn on the radio.

*He does. The static is shrill and jarring. He pounds the radio with his
fist, then gives up and turns it off.*

BRENT: Darn. Sometimes it works and sometimes it doesn't.
SHIRLY: That's OK. It's nice and quiet here.

*Pause. They become aware of the quiet, and it makes them tentative
and nervous, as though they are being watched.*

BRENT: Yeah. It's nice and quiet all right.

Pause. They are groping for conversation.

SHIRLY: Some people are afraid of graveyards. But I think they're nice and quiet.

BRENT: Oh, you can't get more quiet than a graveyard. *Pause.* I mean, if you want quiet, the graveyard is the place to go.

Pause. The tension builds.

SHIRLY: It's nice here.

They stare at each other.

BRENT: Yeah.

SHIRLY: Nice and . . . quiet.

BRENT: Yeah.

Suddenly and without warning, they kiss, passionately. Simultaneously, the brake lights go on and an alto saxophone plays sensuously in the distance, a capella. Near the car, a man lights a cigarette. It is SCREAMIN' JOHN.

SCREAMIN' JOHN:
What we are here to do, Dear Friends
Here behind the Robie Street cemetery
Here in the silence of a quarter to twelve on a Friday night
Is to savour the mixed blessings of First Romance
First Romance as you and I knew it and viewed it
In the Dodge or the Ford or the Chevrolet
Before we became the smooth sophisticates we are today
First Romance for you and me
In all its bite-your-tongue reality
Late at night, some time to kill
Covered in perfume and Clearasil
Oh, we all get the picture
Hit it, boys.

In another part of the stage we see MANNY and CHINK, who have become the background singers for a doo-wop group, starring SCREAMIN' JOHN, singing harmony and dancing 1950s-style choreography. SCREAMIN' JOHN sings the first two verses of "This Could Be the Night":

Twelve o'clock, and no place to go
Park your car, turn up the radio
Your heart is jumpin' because you never know
This could be the night.

Everybody has got to go through it
One time in life, you never quite outgrew it
Once a child, and then before you knew it
This could be the night.

The music stops, abruptly, as do BRENT and SHIRLY. Things are getting a bit too warm for safety.

SHIRLY: Maybe we should, I mean maybe we could try the radio again, OK?
BRENT: Uh, yeah. Sure.

He tries the radio again. There is nothing but static. He pounds the dashboard in frustration.

BRENT: Aw, cripes!

He turns the radio off. Silence. BRENT becomes self-conscious and serious.

BRENT: Listen, Shirly.
SHIRLY: Yeah?
BRENT: I feel like a rat for not being on your side this afternoon.
SHIRLY: *angry* Oh, yeah? Well, that's because you were a rat! You guys set a new standard in rat-ness!
BRENT: I was so scared of looking stupid in front of the guys.

Pause.

SHIRLY: Oh, I don't blame you. Guys can't help it if they're brought up to act like apes. But I don't have to like it, Brent, and if it happens again I'll kick your knees in!
BRENT: *defensive* I don't mean to be disrespectful or anything! Guys don't like being creeps. The creepiness just comes right out of them and they hate it. It's kind of like . . . a skin rash.

Pause. They don't know what to say. Abruptly, they kiss again and the doo-wop music continues, as SCREAMIN' JOHN continues:

SCREAMIN' JOHN:
The weighty matters of First Romance
Don't it make your flesh crawl just to recall
The romance of that kiss by the dashboard light
Of your dad's Buick Special late at night
The sweat, through three layers of Arrid Roll-on
Is drippin' down your ribs and through your shirt
The smell of fear is creepin' past the box of Pepsin

Chiclets you crammed into your mouth half an hour ago
My, my, what a circumstance
Those long-forgotten smells of First Romance.

He sings:

Try and pretend you're older than you are
Tellin' the truth won't get you very far
You're all grown-up because you got a car, and
This could be the night.

BRENT and SHIRLY stop necking, abruptly, scared. The brake lights go out. The music stops.

SHIRLY: I better go home soon. *in panic* What time is it!?
BRENT: *in panic* What? Go home? It's only twelve, I mean, gosh, if that's how it is, if you gotta go home, well . . .
SHIRLY: Maybe it's time we, I mean, maybe it would be better if we, I mean, before it's too late and we go too far, and . . . I don't know what I'm talking about.
BRENT: Neither do I. I mean, gosh Shirly, I hope you don't think that I'm, I mean this isn't something I . . .
SHIRLY: Oh no, it's not like that, it's like, uh . . .
BRENT: Well, if you . . .
SHIRLY: It's kind of . . .
BRENT: Do you want a Chiclet?
SHIRLY: *desperate* Oh, come off it!

They kiss. The brake lights go on. They disappear behind the seat. SCREAMIN' JOHN is watching. The doo-wop chorus picks up tempo, slightly.

SCREAMIN' JOHN
How fragile are the social skills in First Romance
Look back upon the road you went
With pity and embarrassment
For how soon we achieve the gift of the gab, my dears
Be smooth, be sharp, nothing to fear
We are the generation
Of arrogant articulation
Soon enough this is yesterday's news
Who is afraid and who is confused
Soon enough the naked fear will disappear beneath
The bric-a-brac of confident display
But who knows

Maybe the day will dawn when the jaded and the faded
Will turn a hungry eye backward
Will long for another chance
At the sweat, the fear
The reality
Of First Romance

He sings. The music soars.

Nobody told us
What we're in for
Some call it love
Others call it screwin'
Nobody told us
What we're in for
Don't let on that you don't know what you're doin'.

Maybe it's love, maybe infatuation
Some call it romance, some call it degradation
The turning point for every generation
This could be the night, oh yeah
This could be the night, oh my
This could be the night.

The song ends. The brake lights go out. Lights fade to black.

Lights up. MANNY, CHINK, BRENT and SHIRLY are standing and sitting idly about the car from the previous scene. BRENT and SHIRLY are holding hands. MANNY and CHINK are holding quarts of beer, yawning and scratching their arms. It is a typical afternoon in Mushaboom.

MANNY: Biff Mansour?
BRENT: Biffo!
CHINK: Biffaroony!
MANNY: Yeah, well he wants to sell the Ford. Wonder what he wants for it?
BRENT: What are you gonna do with it? Plant flowers in it?
MANNY: *annoyed* Oh, come on!
CHINK: She's been rolled.
MANNY: *concerned* She's been rolled, has she?
CHINK: Heard Biff's gonna put wheels on the roof.

Laughter. MANNY realizes he is being mocked.

BRENT: Every five miles you fill the tank, put in a quart of oil and change the engine.

Laughter.

MANNY: Arrrrrgh!
CHINK: Don't burn gas at all. Got rust holes in the floor you stick your legs through and push it.
BRENT: You gotta push it, Manny.

They push MANNY around a bit. They are always trying to get MANNY to lose his temper, and they always succeed.

MANNY: Aw, c'mon you guys! Quit pickin' on me, will you?

CHINK and BRENT start picking on him.

MANNY: You're always pickin' on me 'cause I'm rich!
BRENT & CHINK: *mock pity* Awwwwwww!
MANNY: Well I didn't ask to be rich, you know!
BRENT & CHINK: Awwwwwww!
MANNY: It was forced on me! *losing his temper* Oh, you nasty, stinking, fishlipped scumbags! You dog turds! You pukes! You . . .

PARKER is standing onstage, watching them. He is very unstylishly dressed because the current fashions won't fit him. He is very ill at ease. MANNY's teasing is abandoned. They have found another straight man.

MANNY: What the hell is that?
CHINK: Who let it out?
PARKER: Hi.
BRENT: Hello, there.
SHIRLY: Hello, Parker.

CHINK and MANNY get up to inspect PARKER. PARKER endures it: he has been through it before.

CHINK: Boy, you're some fat. You always been that fat?
PARKER: Pretty well, yeah.
CHINK: Anybody ever call you Fatso? Piggy? Fats?
MANNY: How about Porky or Blubber?
PARKER: My name is Parker. Donny Parker.

BRENT can't resist.

BRENT: What can we do for you, Mr. Porker?
SHIRLY: Brent!
PARKER: I hear you guys are lookin' for a singer. I wanna try out.

They look at PARKER in silence, then burst into helpless laughter.

PARKER: I'll be seein' you.

PARKER exits. SHIRLY goes after him.

SHIRLY: What a great bunch of guys! I'm so proud of you, Brent!
BRENT: Shirly's right, you guys. Fair's fair, and we gotta give the kid a fair chance even if his appearance is unsuitable.
MANNY: Unsuitable? My God!
CHINK: OK, OK.

SHIRLEY re-enters with PARKER. They regard him for two seconds, then collapse into helpless laughter again.

SHIRLY: I'm leaving. Smells like the sewer backed up.

MANNY, BRENT, CHINK still find all this hilarious. PARKER speaks to them, quietly at first but with growing intensity.

PARKER: Holy cow, are you guys ever witty. It's amazin' how many witty guys you meet when you're . . . when you're heavy. Grade One, you got a bunch of snotty kids with IQ's hoverin' around eighty, and the puns start flyin' soon as the fat kid walks in. Where do they learn that? It's weird. Little League baseball: the fat kid strikes out. "Yah, yah, yah, what did you swing at that one for, fat kid?" What do you think I swung at it for? I wanted to hit a home run, just like you!

He turns on them menacingly. They become a bit alarmed.

What's goin' on here? Are we on TV and I don't know it? Well, whatever it is, you can count me out!

PARKER starts to exit. MANNY, BRENT and CHINK aren't laughing. PARKER stops and turns on them again. He isn't finished.

Boy, are you guys ever thick! You got a band that sounds like old gears shifting! Hell, I could phone in a song, it would sound better than you guys! But that's OK, you witty guys wanna make fat jokes, I'm gettin' out of here because I've heard them all!

PARKER exits. Pause. MANNY, BRENT and CHINK think about this.

CHINK: This is an outburst you don't expect from a fat kid. I vote we give the big fella a chance.
MANNY: I second the motion. Boy, he's some pissed off, eh?

They collapse in laughter, as the lights fade to black. We hear the introduction to "The Fat Boy," an up-tempo R&B tune. A spot hits PARKER, who sings:

Oh ain't the fat boy funny
See him waddle down the street
Make him run ain't that fun
The fat boy ain't no athelete.

But all the time the fat boy's watchin'
There's a smile playin' on his face
In a few more years you'll be laughin' tears
On the other side of your face.

The last laugh is the fat boy's
You will see his point of view
The last laugh is the fat boy's
See the fat boy laugh at you.

So prick up your ears and listen
When the fat boy's talkin' to you
A few more years and a few more beers
And you will be a fat boy too.

And then the last laugh is the fat boy's
You will see his point of view
Oh yeah, the last laugh is the fat boy's
See the fat boy laugh at you.

Youth and beauty are fickle friends
Like vanity and pride
Wake up one day, they've gone away
They're fightin' for the other side
The fat boy sees it early
So it comes as no surprise
When he finds that he's older
The hair's on his shoulder
And the age is in his eyes.

The last laugh is the fat boy's
You will see his point of view
The last laugh is the fat boy's
See the fat boy laugh at you.

You'll be old and fat and ugly
You'll make all the young girls sick
You'll be lots of fun when you try and run
It's just a matter of arithmetic.

Oh yeah, the last laugh is the fat boy's
You will see his point of view
The last laugh is the fat boy's
See the fat boy laugh at you.

End song. Blackout, except for a single spot on PARKER. The Monarchs play a series of power chords. Lights up on the whole band, with PARKER as lead singer. The following is narrated, played and sung, as though the band were at a dance. The lights are flashing and they are sounding very good.

PARKER: Six o'clock on Saturday, November 30, 1960. Manny's old lady's 1960 Chev Impala convertible screeches to a stop in front of our house. Jeez Murphy, am I ever excited! I'm playin' in the Monarchs and I'm gettin' paid, and here they are to pick me up and we're goin' to the Moncton Arena for my first job. The biggest day in my life. I get into the car with Manny, Brent, Chink, a Fender Telecaster, a Fender Bassman, two Bandmaster amps, two Electrovoice microphones, two P.A. speakers, a set of Ludwig drums . . . and two cases of Bright's Winette, a sweet white wine made in Hildon, Nova Scotia, affordably priced at a dollar five a bottle.

The band breaks into a rhythmic up-tempo vamp, which continues underneath the following.

The tires squeal and in ten minutes we're tearin' down the Trans Canada at eighty miles an hour, screamin' at the top of our lungs for no reason at all. We hit Moncton at a quarter to eight, with a lot less Winette than we started with. We unload the gear and set it up in the Arena. The thing is used as a hockey rink, so it's pretty impressive. I'm nervous. We check the sound, then go back to the car for a little more Winette. By eight-thirty everybody's drunk and irritable and ready to rock and roll!

The band goes into an up-tempo rock number.

We start playin' to about fifty people, but by ten the place is . . .

PARKER: *singing*
  Slippin' and a-slidin'
  Peekin' and a-hidin'
  Been told a long time ago
  Slippin' and a-slidin'
  Peekin' and a hidin'
  Been told a long time ago
  I been told
  Now baby now you've been bold
  I won't be your fool no more.

  We call a short break for refreshment, then we reel back onstage
  for "Lucille," "Sittin' in Ya-Ya," and . . .

He sings:

  Keep a-knockin' but you can't come in
  Keep a-knockin' but you can't come in
  Keep a-knockin' but you can't come in
  Come back tomorrow night and try again.

  We're startin' to run out of songs, but we can just play the same
  songs over again and who cares anyway? We're really feelin' good.
  They're all jivin' and yellin' like we're stars or somethin', and
  we're playin' "SAVED," and I'm screamin' . . .

He sings:

  I used to lie
  I used to cheat
  I used to lie, cheat, step on people's feet
  I used to lie and cheat
  Lie and cheat and step on people's feet
  But now I'm steppin' on glory
  Beatin' on that big bass drum

  I'm screamin' and rollin' around on the floor, and the crowd is
  all around yellin' and fannin' me with their handkerchiefs, and
  we're all sweatin' like a bunch of pigs and havin' ourselves a real
  good time.

The band launches into a waltz. PARKER sings:

  Remember, in your search
  For fortune and fame
  You may travel this whole world

This whole wide domain
But I'm tellin' you, I'm tellin' you
That you'll never find
A true love like I see for you
In your darling's eyes
Go on home
Go on home.

Then it's the home waltz. I can hardly stand up. Six hundred people are waltzin' out there, and you could be in Las Vegas or Hollywood or Europe, but you wouldn't find a more romantic spot, like the old Moncton Arena, on that Saturday night.

The band breaks into the rhythmic up-tempo vamp we heard while they were travelling to Moncton.

We load up the car and squeal the tires out of Moncton, and by the time we hit the Trans Canada we're doin' a hundred and ten and I'm not . . . feelin' too hot. In fact, I think I'm gonna puke. Right now. I say, "Listen you guys, you gotta stop the car 'cause I think I'm gonna puke!"
MANNY: Forget it! No way!
PARKER: They don't believe me. Chink hands me the bottle, and I get a whiff of that old Winette, and I just get the window down on my side of the car, and . . . AWAY WE GO!!!

The band plays appropriate music as PARKER turns his back to the audience and mimes a series of nasty heaves, recovers, then turns back to the audience, looking a bit green.

I don't know if you've ever puked out of a car window doin' a hundred and ten, but I'll tell you one thing. It won't stay outside the car. It whips back in all over us!
MANNY: Arrrrrrrgh!
PARKER: In fact, there's a fair-sized pool of it nestled in the well behind the back seat where the convertible top's supposed to go.
MANNY: Son of a bitch!
PARKER: Manny naturally resents this, because his mother's supposed to take the car to church tomorrow morning. Ah, but pretty soon we're all hootin' and laughin' about the whole thing, tearin' down the highway at a hundred and ten miles an hour!

The music becomes quite furious, then softens.

By the time they get me home it's nearly six in the morning, and I never had so much fun in my whole life.

The music becomes lyrical as the lights dim to a single spot on PARKER. SCREAMIN' JOHN lights a cigarette in another part of the stage as PARKER mimes watching the car go away. We hear a soft boogie on piano, and a bit of alto sax. SCREAMIN' JOHN narrates PARKER's drunken jouney to bed, and PARKER mimes accordingly across the empty stage.

SCREAMIN' JOHN:
   What a night it's been
   You tell Manny to drop you off at the corner and you say a little
      prayer
   That he won't squeal his tires when he takes off out of there
   Because it will be a very rocky morning if you wake up the folks
      stinkin' of cigarettes and wine and puke
   Three hours before Sunday School
   Sunday is never so sacred as it is to the underage drunk
   The drunk will be punished without mercy or warning
   Who shatters the silence of Sunday morning
   Doors are approached with the delicacy of a surgeon
   Open and close, with gentle urgin'
   Careful sneaking, no clicking and creaking
   Off with those shoes and when you're done
   Slide those socks over the linoleum
   Then through the hall
   Past the photograph of Grandpa and the curling trophies
   Past the matador and the ballerina on the wall
   Past the crystal ball you turn over to make it snow
   And the souvenir of Mexico
   Past the window with the stained glass
   And the lamp you made in manual training class
   Into the bathroom
   Hit the side of the bowl when you start to piss
   So the world won't hear that tell-tale hiss
   Take it easy, don't rush it
   And for God's sake don't forget
   Don't flush it
   Into the bedroom
   Get those clothes off, don't jingle your change
   Pray the furniture ain't been re-arranged
   Slip between flannelette sheets . . .

Get a look at the sun as it starts to rise
Yellin' good morning through the window
Echoin' off the mirror, and the stray pennies
And the fake sapphire cufflinks
And . . .
Close your eyes.

SCREAMIN' JOHN sings a lullaby, as PARKER sleeps.

And the sun shone, straight and strong
For everyone to see
On masonic dignitaries
Retired missionaires
Hallelujas and hail Marys
The temperate and the wary
But none but the very, very
Drunk
Was there to see . . .

The lullaby becomes a reprise of "Just a Memory." SCREAMIN' JOHN sings:

Don't you know it's just a memory
Got no particular reality
Think of it as just a fantasy
It was so long ago.
It was so long ago.
It was so long ago.

Blackout.

Act Two

Lights up. The Monarchs are onstage, playing the introduction to "King of Friday Night." Five years have gone by, and the band is much improved and much more confident. They are wearing band uniforms of the period, and perform choreography and extended solos. They have more equipment. And PARKER is definitely the star.

Got no time for a life of crime
We got everything we need
Got no use for the hangman's noose
Or the sins of hate and greed
Ain't so hard to clean your own backyard
Yeah, the secret is in sight
The bird has flown when you're on your own
And you're the king of Friday night.

Folks grow old tryin' to save their souls
With their money in the bank
Lost their mind and they're deaf and blind
And they don't know who to thank
We escaped without a scrape
Now everything's all right
Little sins ain't worth fallin' in
When you're the king of Friday night.

Life's so hard, Daddy told me
And I know my Daddy thought he was right
Life's so hard, Daddy told me
But he weren't the king of Friday
Weren't the king of Friday
Weren't the king of Friday night.

Ooo we're the king of Friday night
The king of Friday night
Ooo we're the king of Friday night
The king of Friday night.

We may grow old and we may grow cold
And scared and stiff and fat
We may turn thirty with minds so dirty
That we don't know where it's at

131

We won't care 'cause we once was there
And even though it may sound trite
We'll be young again when we remember when
We were the king of Friday night.

Life's so hard, Daddy told me
And I know my daddy thought he was right
Life's so hard, Daddy told me
But he weren't the king of Friday
Weren't the king of Friday
Weren't the king of Friday night.

Ooo we're the king of Friday night
The king of Friday
Ooo we're the king of Friday night
The king of Friday night.

The song ends with a flashy series of instrumental breaks and choreography. Blackout, followed immediately by a spotlight on SHIRLY, who is standing on one side of the stage. She speaks, accompanied by a solo piano playing the introduction to "Wish I Could Sing."

SHIRLY: They're some good, aren't they? Best band in Nova Scotia, everyone knows that. When the Monarchs are playing you can forget your Bingo and hockey and wrestling 'cause everyone's going to be at the dance. It's been like that for five years now. Five years and I've been going to every dance. Oh, I know Brent and I go together, but I would have come anyway. I just love the music, that's all.

General stage lighting fades up, dimly. BRENT is at the edge of the stage, counting the money and putting it into five piles for distribution. MANNY and CHINK watch him closely. PARKER is sitting apart from the others, thinking.

You know, it's funny, but I sometimes think I'm closer to the music listening to it than they are playing it. Look at them. Chink and Manny are talking about who they'll jump in the car tonight. Brent's estimating gross receipts. And Parker's thinking about being a star. The music really isn't the important thing. They're too busy planning and dreaming and fighting to really listen. Isn't that sad? I wouldn't be like that. If I could sing, I wouldn't think about anything else. I mean, if you can't be happy singing, how can you ever be happy at all?

She sings "Wish I Could Sing":

Don't wanna be no secretary
I don't wanna learn to type
Don't wanna wear no wedding dress
And marry Mr. Right
I got nothin' against no women
Don't misunderstand
I just wanna be a singer
In a dancin' band.

Wish I could sing
Oh, I wish I could sing
You can stuff homes and gardens
And your wedding ring
Just wish I could sing
Life is so easy for those who can sing
Life is so easy for those who can sing.

SHIRLY continues to hum, a capella, as the lights come up full.

MANNY: Shirly! We're trying to count the money.

BRENT is completing the division of the money. SHIRLY shrugs and joins them. CHINK indicates one of the piles.

CHINK: What's that extra pile there for? Someone in the Monarchs I don't know about?

BRENT: Aw, gosh, Chink, do we have to go through that every night? It's expenses.

CHINK: Expenses? Jeez Murphy look at the size of that pile! When can we expect delivery of the Lear jet?

BRENT: Come on, Chink, somebody's gotta pay Manny for gas. It's his car and it's his truck and it's the only fair thing to do, OK?

MANNY: No shit monkey, and don't you forget it or next time you *walk* to Yarmouth!

CHINK: Listen to him! Talkin' about fair when he already owns half the province! Old D.B. must really be prayin' for you since the heart attack! Ain't that typical? Rich to friggin' richer! And off his friends, that's what kills me! I'm the best friend the bastard's got and he's syphonin' food from my mouth! What an asshole!

MANNY can take no more. He goes for CHINK, out of control. CHINK takes evasive action, and BRENT steps in immediately out of long practice.

MANNY: You snot! You puke! You lipless, turd-faced son of a whore!

CHINK: Keep him away from me, Brent! Keep him away!

MANNY: Let me at him, Brent! Just let me at him this once and his big mouth is comin' right off his face!

BRENT: Cut it out, guys, cut it out! Chink, shut up! *to CHINK* Manny's only gettin' gas money and you know it, so stop needling him! *to MANNY* Manny, sit down, you know what he's like.

They calm down a bit.

CHINK: Yeah, well that pile still looks pretty big to me.

BRENT: Shut up, Chink!

MANNY: Shut up!

CHINK: Yeah, yeah, shut up. This band's turnin' Nazi. No free expression.

BRENT: Shut up, Chink!

MANNY: Shut up!

SHIRLY: You guys are charming company.

CHINK: Shut up, Shirly.

BRENT: Shut up, Chink!

MANNY: Why doesn't everybody just shut up!

PARKER: Can I say something? We got a practice tomorrow at two, remember? We learn "Hold On, I'm Comin'" and "Walk That Walk."

CHINK: Practice? Aw, Jeez Murphy, see what I mean? We're practisin' like a bunch of Nazis!

MANNY: Cripes Parker, we just had a practice, shit, just . . .

PARKER: Two months ago. We learned three songs and remembered two at the next dance. A week later we forgot one more.

BRENT: Listen Parker, I'm busy at the office so I can't make it. Sorry. You gotta remember that Manny and I are working days now, so we're gonna have to wait for a day off, OK?

MANNY: Maybe we'll practise next week, Parker.

CHINK: Or the week after that.

MANNY: Or the week after that.

MANNY and CHINK giggle as money is handed out.

BRENT: I think the Rotary Club is stealin' money from us again.

MANNY: You're kidding! My God, can't you trust anyone?

CHINK: What's that? The Rotary Club?

PARKER: Listen you guys, I been pushin' for a practice for two weeks now, and I'm not gettin' too much enthusiasm, and I don't wanna be too much of a drag, so I'm quitting the band as of tonight, and I'm goin' away in a couple of weeks.

A long pause as the others digest this. Everything becomes quiet.

BRENT: Do you really mean that, Parker?

PARKER: Yeah.

MANNY: C'mon, Parker, you don't do you?

PARKER: Yeah, Manny.

MANNY: Shitstick.

BRENT: Gosh.

PARKER: You guys have lost interest. Brent, you're with Barkhouse Insurance; Manny, you're investin' and stuff. Chink . . . well, you're retired. You guys wanna play as a kind of hobby, a little extra money, a good time on the weekends. You're not keepin' up. Gee Manny, remember you said the Beatles were a fad like hula hoops?

MANNY: I still think it's a stupid name. Not even spelled right.

BRENT: Manny, this is serious. Parker says he's quittin' the band.

MANNY: Wants to be King Shit. Wants to go to college or something.

CHINK: Aw shit, Parker, what are you tryin' to do to me? You're makin' money. You'll never have more friends or a better time than you got here. What do you wanna quit the band for?

PARKER: You guys don't have a clue what I'm talkin' about, do you? I'm pointin' out that there's life beyond Mushaboom. There are more exciting things to do besides squealing your tires down Provost Street and gettin' drunk in the Legion. There's people out there who don't care what kind of a car you got or who's screwin' who. They don't care about that kind of stuff and I wanna be one of them, OK?

Pause.

PARKER: I guess I better be goin'. See you.

PARKER exits.

BRENT: Now what was that all about?

SHIRLY: Maybe he's sayin' he's almost twenty and he can't get a girl in this town so he's goin' someplace where he can.

MANNY *to CHINK* You know that could be it! I know this slut in Bass River with bazongers out to here...

SHIRLY: Or maybe he's sayin' this town isn't good enough for him.

MANNY: Now what's that's supposed to mean?

SHIRLY: Think about it, Manny.

MANNY: Think about what?

SHIRLY: Just think about it, Manny!

MANNY: Think about what?

SHIRLY: Think about it! Use your pea-brain!

CHINK: That ain't the point! What are we gonna do? We're up shit's creek without a singer.

BRENT: I don't know, Chink.

Pause. SHIRLY wants to say something, but thinks better of it.

CHINK: C'mon! Think! What're we gonna do?

MANNY: You know, I think we've had it.

CHINK: Had it? Had what? What's that supposed to mean?

BRENT: Manny's sayin' he thinks the band's gonna break up. Maybe he's right. Look, this is all pretty sudden. Maybe Parker will change his mind.

SHIRLY: Oh sure he will. Tomorrow he'll decide he just *loves* it here.

BRENT: Well we can talk about it tomorrow. C'mon, Shirly.

Exit BRENT and SHIRLY. Pause.

MANNY: Hey Chink, wanna get drunk or screwed or something?

CHINK: Naw. Get out of here. Leave me alone.

MANNY: What'd I ever do to you, anyway?

CHINK: Look. You got money and I don't. We're from the same town but we're from different planets. OK?

MANNY is hurt.

MANNY: OK.

MANNY exits. Pause.

CHINK: Oh shit, what am I gonna do? I'm gonna have to get a job!

Fast fade to black.

In the darkness we hear a wailing alto sax. Lights come up slowly to reveal that we are in the cemetery again, with the same night sky we saw in the Brent-Shirly cemetery scene. There is also the '59 Chevrolet, except that now it has been turned around so that the front of the car is facing the audience. The front of the car is a tangled wreck. In the car lounges SCREAMIN' JOHN, smoking a cigarette. The piano plays soft boogie music as he speaks to the audience.

SCREAMIN' JOHN:
Well, hello there, my friends
No doubt those perceptive eyes will recognize
The austere grandeur of the Robie Street cemetery
As you have surmised there is more activity than meets the eyes
For as the years go by for you and me we come to value
Our privacy
And if you live in a small Canadian town
Where you're known on the street by everyone you meet
There's little privacy to be found
So in moments of great joy or despair many of us repair
To the Robie Street cemetery
Where all eyes are closed
Oh, there's a bit of view to the south of the Salmon River
Lazily makin' its way to the Bay of Fundy
Carryin' all the crap from D.B.'s hat factory
It's a pretty sight this time of night
With the sun settin' behind the neon of Frank Langille's used car
   lot
Ain't it ironic that, when we look for privacy
We go where someday we'll have all the privacy we ever wanted.

He has a good laugh over that one.

Oh, I know there are those who say it's haunted
But it ain't haunted by those who have passed on
This place is haunted by living refugees
Hidin' from the big blue eyes
Of small town publicity.

Lights come up a bit to reveal scattered gravestones onstage, made from the reverse side of band speaker boxes. Among the gravestones are BRENT and SHIRLY. We hear crickets. SCREAMIN' JOHN watches.

BRENT: It's nice here.

SHIRLY: Nice and quiet.

BRENT: Yeah.

SHIRLY: *laughing* Remember the first time we came here together? It seems like so long ago.

BRENT: It's been years and years.

SHIRLY: We were so young then. It's hard to remember what it was like, being that young.

BRENT: I'd just got my driver's licence. Sixteen.

SHIRLY: Sixteen. With pimples.

BRENT: Sixteen. We were just getting the band going. Now it's all over.

SHIRLY: You can't fight something like that. It's like the measles.

BRENT: Yeah, it had to happen. You can't play in a rock and roll band all your life. You've got to make something of yourself sooner or later.

SHIRLY: Sooner or later.

BRENT: And I'm getting pretty busy. I'm doing claims you know, and Mr. Barkhouse himself says that it'll only be a couple of years before I'm a qualified adjuster.

SHIRLY: Adjuster. Somehow, that word always makes me think of hernias.

BRENT: Shirly, the band isn't everything. Insurance can be a lot of fun, too.

SHIRLY: Hmmmmmm.

BRENT: OK Shirly, let's stop kidding ourselves. This is awful, and I feel just terrible. I've been working my way up all my life thinking that the Monarchs were just some kind of a hobby. Now I see that it's the only interesting thing I ever did. Or ever will do. I'm a dull person, Shirly! Can you imagine how it feels to know that? To find yourself humming along with elevator music? To know that you enjoy washing the car, whether it's dirty or not? I'm a dull person, Shirly! I'm the kind of guy who plays golf! I don't know if I can face that.

Pause. They walk in the graveyard. They hold hands. SCREAMIN' JOHN watches.

SHIRLY: There's such a lot of graves. Seems like a lot more than there were five years ago. Look. There's Mrs. Tupper's, remember? She taught math in Grade Seven.

BRENT: She just keeled over one day in class.

SHIRLY: Yeah. And there's Parker's dad. Remember? He just got thinner and thinner and then he died. It nearly killed Parker's mom. And there's Kathy Burns. She was my best friend when we were fourteen. Then she got sick and died and we don't know why. I still can't listen to "Teen Angel" without crying.

BRENT: Yeah. A lot of people are dead now, that weren't dead before.

Pause.

Screamin' John McGee's just down the road a bit.

SCREAMIN' JOHN perks up. A spotlight fades up on him as he sits in the car, miming the following speech to rhythmic, menacing music.

SHIRLY: Yeah. They say that was some accident. They say he did it on purpose. They said he was doin' a hundred and ten when he hit that pole on Woodlawn Avenue.

BRENT: Yeah. Sliced right through it. Then he hit Dr. Mosher's Cadillac parked in front of the house. Then a fire hydrant. Then the Creelmans' station wagon. Then he wiped out the Lantzes' front porch. Crushed the TV set in the living-room. When Screamin' John did it, he really did it good.

SCREAMIN' JOHN takes a bow, then settles back in the wrecked car. We hear crickets again.

SHIRLY: Most spectacular accident Mushaboom ever saw.

BRENT: Screamin' John was crazy. They said you couldn't let him anywhere near a cat. He'd tear the legs . . .

SHIRLY: Right off it.

BRENT: Yeah.

Pause. He makes up his mind.

Shirly, we've been going together for a number of years now.

SHIRLY: I'll say! This signet ring is so heavy my right arm is two inches longer than my left. And the adhesive tape is filthy!

BRENT: Shirly, I'm tryin' to talk to you about something.

Music. BRENT and SHIRLY sing "Normal People," a gentle ballad:

BRENT:
Could you stand it, living here
And not in Italy
All around you nothing but
Familiarity

In this familiar town
With this familiar man
When all your friends are gone
And sending postcards from Japan
Could you stand it here?

SHIRLY:
Could you stand it, living here
With this familiar face
Would you long for movie stars
With dresses made of lace
Just this familiar woman
With nothing much to say
Nothing too spectacular
And older every day
Could you stand it here?

BRENT & SHIRLY:
Could we live our lives like normal people
Living for today
Three kids, a dog, a TV set
Two mortgages to pay
Maybe even ordinariness
Can't take our love away
Normal people, living in the world
Normal people, living in the world
Normal people, living in the world.

SHIRLY and BRENT kiss, then exit arm-in-arm as MANNY enters from the other side of the stage. SCREAMIN' JOHN watches as MANNY looks about to make certain he is not being watched, then kneels down to pray.

MANNY: Dear Lord. M. Bridgeman again. It is at times of change that we turn to You for guidance. There are times in life when an old way dieth and a new way must come to take its place. These times are upon me Lord, and I know not what to do. I am a man at the crossroads. Like St. Paul, several roads stretcheth out before me, and I know not where to turn. I ask Thy guidance. Should I take the path of real estate as D.B. advises, or is stocks and bonds more in keeping with current market trends? Or perhaps Kentucky Fried Chicken holds the answer, as Thou knowest what a growth industry that is! Help me choose shrewdly Lord, for if I am a failure D.B. will haunt me to my grave and beyond!

Inherited wealth is my cross, Lord. Help me to endure Chink, who resents my station in life and taunts me without mercy. He just doesn't like me! I've known that guy all my life and he doesn't like me! Give me guidance, Lord. Should I give his mother a raise?

Lord, I ask for guidance in my home life. Help me to choose a wife wisely: one that lacketh not in physical charms but naggeth me not about my drinking. Let my house be somewhat large, with a small pool. Let my children be nicer than me. Spare me such diseases as cancer and heart disease, and spare my liver. Grant me a long and restful retirement, with frequent trips to Florida. Let me die peacefully in my sleep. Please understand, Lord, I am aware that my requests suck. They are unworthy and material-istic, but what are you gonna do? It's what everyone else is pray-ing for. I'm not unique, only rich. Forgive me. This has been a nice frank discussion, Lord. Thanks for everything. Amen.

MANNY takes a pint of lemon gin from his back pocket and drinks from it as he exits. Meanwhile, CHINK enters from the other side of the stage, very upset.

CHINK: Isn't that a bitch! My life's all over, I just can't believe it! Yesterday I was the hottest thing in Mushaboom and now look at me! No talent, no money, I haven't even got a suit! An old man with nothing but my memories, and I ain't even twenty-one!

He starts to cry.

Aw goddamn it, how come it's all goin' by so fast? Ain't there no brakes on this thing? Can't we enjoy something for a second without it turning to shit in front of our eyes? What's the point??? What am I gonna do???

Spotlight on SCREAMIN' JOHN as he lights a cigarette.

SCREAMIN' JOHN: Boo.
CHINK: Aw, shut up.

SCREAMIN' JOHN screams, very scary, for effect.

SCREAMIN' JOHN: Aaaaaaaaaah!!
CHINK: *terrified* Aaaaaaaaaah!!
SCREAMIN' JOHN: That's better.
CHINK: Screamin' John!
SCREAMIN' JOHN: As you live and breathe.
CHINK: I'll be goddamned!
SCREAMIN' JOHN: I wouldn't go as far as all that.

CHINK: I'm gonna puke! You're a ghost. You know that, don't you?

SCREAMIN' JOHN: It's crossed my mind. Consider me a reminder
of things behind.

CHINK: What are you gettin' at?

SCREAMIN' JOHN: Take this advice: when life starts to take its toll
First you rock, and then you roll.

CHINK: And just what the fuck is that supposed to mean?

*We hear ethereal music building to a doo-wop chorus. A spot isolates
SCREAMIN' JOHN as he speaks to the audience as though it were
Chink.*

SCREAMIN' JOHN:
You been playin' it for five years and you
Don't know the meaning of what you hear
Well I'm gonna tell you
When you're lookin' good and feelin' fine
Havin' fun and in your prime
That's when you rock
You rock all day, you rock all night
You rock on, with no end in sight
Forget the future, forget the past
You rock on while the rockin' lasts
But there comes a time when the rockin's done
You've lost the beat, you've lost the fun
So you change the beat to save your soul
When you can't rock, that's when you roll
You roll along when the wind is strong
And it's blowin' you off your feet
You roll along when you can't be strong
Till you've found a brand new beat
Join me in this little number, will you?

*Lights up. MANNY, BRENT, and CHINK are onstage. They join
SCREAMIN' JOHN as backup chorus and dancers to "You Better Rock,
You Better Roll."*

Doo-wop-wop
Doo-wop-wop
Diddy diddy diddy yeah
Doo-wop-wop
Diddy diddy diddy yeah
When you're in the pit
And you're full of shit

And you don't know what to do
When you can't relate
'Cause you're two years late
And you've missed your rendezvous
(Yes you have, dit dit dit dit dit dit dit)
Missed your rendezvous, wop-wop
Doo-wop-wop, diddy diddy diddy
Ooooooh, doo-dah
Ooooooh, oh, yeah

Dit dit dit dit dit dit
Dit dit dit dit dit dit
Dit dit dit dit dit dit
Dit dit dit dit dit dit
Rendezvous, yeah!

Doo-wop-wop
Doo-wop-wop
Diddy diddy diddy yeah
Doo-wop-wop
Doo-wop-wop
Diddy diddy diddy yeah
When your mind is dumb
And your heart is numb
And you're falling down the hole
When it's time to face the music
You better rock
You better roll.

You better rock
You better roll
When the situation's out of control
When the situation's out of control
You better rock
You better roll.

Stop playin' that waltz
'Cause it's got its faults
And it ain't so sweet no more
And your favourite rhumba
Is now a bumma
And they laughin' you off the floor
Put last year's hits
In the garbage pit

'Cause the gold has turned to coal
When it's time to face the music
You better rock
You better roll.

You better rock
You better roll
When the situation's out of control
When the situation's out of control
You better rock
You better roll.

*The doo-wop chorus continues over a saxophone solo. SCREAMIN'
JOHN ascends to heaven. BRENT, MANNY and CHINK dance offstage as the lights fade. As soon as the lights go to black, a spotlight
hits SHIRLY in another part of the stage. She sings "The Common Complaint," to piano accompaniment:*

When I was just a little girl
I asked my mother what's wrong with me
Why can't I be famous
Why can't I be rich
Here's what she said to me:

Que sera sera
You can't be what you ain't
It's the common complaint
Of the common young man
Que sera sera
Think you're different, you ain't
Be it sinner or saint
You'll just be what you can.

*The light on SHIRLY fades as she exits. Lights up in another part of
the stage. The night sky, the gravestones and the car have disappeared.
PARKER is alone onstage, sitting in a chrome-and-plastic kitchen chair.
He speaks to the audience as though to his mother, reacting to her
unheard replies.*

PARKER: What? No thanks, Mom, no more for me. . . . No
really, Mom, it was great pie, but . . . No Mom, I'm feelin' fine,
it's just . . . Mom, no kidding, two pieces is enough and I've
already had two, and . . . no! Not three pieces! Not five or ten
either! Two pieces! Enough! . . . Well OK, Mom, maybe just a
sliver . . . Aw, goddamn it, Mom, you just gave me half the

damned pie, and didn't I just tell you . . . I'm sorry Mom, I didn't mean to swear at you. I just wish you would listen to me, that's all.

Pause.

Listen Mom, I've gotta talk to you about something. I wanna tell you that I've quit the band, and . . . Well I'm real glad that makes you happy Mom, but it doesn't mean I'm takin' over the store full time. No, I'm not. I've been savin' my money for a while, and . . . Yeah, I know, Dad was a great saver, but will you listen? . . . I know, I know, Dad was a fine man and it's been hard with him gone but I'm talkin' about me now. I'm goin' away, Mom . . .
Now look, Mom, don't panic! Fred can run the store, he's early fourteen, and . . . aw look Mom, it's nothin' but Mars bars and cigarettes and a cash register, so don't go talkin' to me like it was the Bank of Commerce! Now will you hear me out? OK. You still listenin'? OK.

Pause.

Mom, I wanna go away. I wanna go someplace a whole lot different than Mushaboom because I wanna be something a whole lot different than me. Ever since I can remember, I've always been the fat kid on the block, and . . . Thin out?? Who says I'm gonna thin out?? You've been tellin' me I'm gonna thin out for sixteen years now, and there's been no sign of it yet! Mom, no kidding, as long as I'm in Mushaboom I'll always be the fat kid who sings, and that ain't what I wanna be! I wanna be great! I wanna be fantastic! And I can't be that here in a million years. So I'm gettin' out and I'm goin' to Toronto.

Pause.

Aw Mom, what do you wanna do that for? Aw c'mon, Mom, stop it. Yeah, I know. It's been hard . . . But I'm goin'. I'm goin' away, and there's nothin' you can do about it. And you know there's nothin' I can do about it, either.

Pause.

Well, I thought I'd take the train. It only costs twenty-three dollars, if you sit up.

Pause.

Yeah, I know, Mom, it would be a whole lot different if he was here. Yeah, I know, Mom. Yeah. I know.

The piano is playing the introduction to "Mom and Dad." PARKER sings:

They went to school together
She wore hats with feathers
He wore suits
He sang every Sunday
She worked at the women's institute
And straight meant no lying
And gay meant no crying
And high was in the air
Let others long for famous faces
Look for famous places
They don't care.

But it's sad and it's true
Mom and Dad, I'll never be like you
Oh yes
It's sad and it's true
Couldn't do it if I wanted to.

Didn't know what for
But he went off to war
Full of pride
He came back a whole lot older
Arms reached out to hold her
Nothing to hide
All those years I never heard
A single unkind word
Pass between you two
How's it so easy to be good and kind
What I find hard to find
Just came to you.

But it's sad and it's true
Mom and Dad, I'll never be like you
Oh yes
It's sad and it's true
Couldn't do it if I wanted to
Oh yes
It's sad and it's true

Mom and Dad
I'll never be
Like you.

*Lights fade to black. In the darkness we hear the voice of SCREAMIN'
JOHN, singing a slow reprise of "Just a Memory." There is a ghostly
light on him as he sings:*

Don't you know its just a memory
Got no particular reality
Oh, a foggy memory
It was so long ago
It was so long ago
It was so long ago.

*Lights up, bright. The stage is set for the reunion concert. There are
balloons and a banner. MANNY is alone onstage, pacing the floor in
a band uniform, looking at his big gold watch, nearly insane.*

MANNY: Sweet crucified jumpin' German Jesus! Am I the only
  member of the Monarchs who can afford a goddamn watch? Am
  I the only one who's ever, ever, ever on time? Ten minutes to
  go! No! Eight! Eight minutes! I can hear them shuffling their feet
  out there! I think I'm goin' out of my mind.

Enter BRENT in an identical jacket, with a sense of urgency.

BRENT: We got trouble.
MANNY: Trouble? Oh no, not trouble!!
BRENT: Chink won't go on.
MANNY: What do you mean, he won't go on?
BRENT: Is there another meaning? Chink won't go on. He's in the
  john.
MANNY: Uh-huh.
BRENT: Says we're not gonna trample on his memories.
MANNY: Oh, yeah.
BRENT: Says he wants to grow old gracefully.
MANNY: The bastard! His final revenge!

PARKER enters over this outburst.

PARKER: We better tune up. I think she's ready to go.
MANNY: Yeah, and we got trouble.
PARKER: Trouble? Oh no, not trouble.
BRENT: Chink refuses to play. He's in the crapper.

MANNY: Doesn't want us to trample on his memories! I'll trample on his memories! I'll trample on his face!

Enter SHIRLY, excited, in a lovely dress.

SHIRLY: Well, we're sold out, the doors are closed, and we're ready to go.
PARKER: We got trouble
SHIRLY: Oh no, not trouble!
BRENT: It's a crisis. Chink's in the men's room and he won't come out. He's sitting on the commode with his pants down.
PARKER: Maybe he's having a crap.
MANNY: No, he isn't! Six months of planning, that's what's going down the toilet! I'll sue the bastard, that'll give him a memory!
SHIRLY: Hold on a minute, will you?

SHIRLY exits.

MANNY: Where is she going? Was it something I said?
PARKER: I don't know, Manny! How should I know?
BRENT: We better tune up, just in case.

BRENT tunes his guitar. MANNY goes to the edge of the stage.

MANNY: Listen to those feet. Three thousand feet at six dollars a pair. Expectant feet! Feet that have come miles, just for this event! I think I'm going hysterical, boys!

Enter SHIRLY with CHINK in tow against his will. He is fastening his belt.

CHINK: Son of a bitch! Isn't anything sacred any more? She came right into the men's room, Brent! I was sitting on the commode!
MANNY: Shirly, Shirly, Shirly . . .
SHIRLY: Shut up and get yourselves together, will you? I'm losing my patience.
PARKER: What's gotten into you, Chink?
CHINK: Look at me, Parker! I'm nothin'! I got this thing in my mind that I was really somethin' once, what's wrong with that? Look, my present's a mess, do we have to shit all over my past too? Oh goddamn it . . .

CHINK starts to cry. BRENT moves as though to comfort him.

BRENT: Chink, shut up. You think you're the only failure around here? You think I like adjusting insurance? I am so boring, I nod off just thinking about myself! And what about Parker here? You

148

think his life's ambition was to be the Wayne Newton of the North?

MANNY: Yeah, and what about me? D.B. left me four million dollars. I made some shrewd investments, now I got three and a half. Christ, we're all failures! You gotta learn to relax and enjoy it!

SHIRLY: Will you guys just shut up? While you're working out the meaning of your lives, there are a lot of people out there who think you're more important than the Beatles, and that may not be enough for you, but you're not going to let them down! You're going to take a rare couple of hours and think about someone else for a change! This isn't for you! It's for them!

MANNY: That was very well put, Shirly.

SHIRLY: Now get ready! Do you have any idea what time it is? And another thing . . .

As she speaks the band is in a great hurry to get changed and to get their instruments on. Spot on SHIRLY as she sings a slow reprise of "The Boys' Club" to piano accompaniment:

Cruel is a virtue
Gentle is a sin
No matter how they hurt you
Gotta play to win
As long as you're a girl
They'll never let you in
At the boys' club, oh yeah
At the boys' club, oh yeah
The boys' . . .

MANNY: Shirly?

SHIRLY: What?

MANNY: Shirly, on behalf of the band I'd like to ask if you'll sing with us tonight.

SHIRLY: You mean it?

MANNY: Yeah.

Blackout. Drum roll. We hear the voice of SCREAMIN' JOHN.

SCREAMIN' JOHN: Ladies and Gentlemen, it's Friday night in Mushaboom, Nova Scotia, and the Monarchs are back!!

Lights up. It is very colourful. The Monarchs, plus SHIRLY, sing a medley of the major songs in Rock and Roll. *The band is in heaven.*

Well its a-one for your money
Two for your soul
Three for your sanity
Now rock and roll

Have you got a lot of urges in your body
That you can't control
Get yourself in motion, and
Play a little rock and roll.

Has your heart been hocked
Have your memories all been stoie
Get yourself in motion, and
Play a little rock and roll.

Well your hands are shakin'
Your guts are achin'
You can't stop cryin' 'cause
Your heart's just achin'
Your mind is bitchin'
Your insides are itchin'
While your daddy's in the office, and
Your momma's in the kitchen.

Gotta do somethin'
To save your doggone soul
Get yourself in motion, and
Play a little rock and roll
Get yourself in motion, and
Play a little rock and roll
Get yourself in motion, and
Play a little rock and roll.

The music continues. BRENT takes a solo.

SHIRLY: *to audience* I've never seen anything like it! When the
music started you'd have thought the ghost of Screamin' John
appeared, 'cause a roar went up from the crowd like nothing I've
ever heard!

Key and tempo change. The band plays "You're Gonna Be a Star":

Gonna play some rock and roll
Just for kicks
Household Finance will lend
The money real quick

Get yourself a booking in
The Legion Hall
Everybody's gonna have a ball.

You're gonna be a star
Oh, yes you are
You play your cheap guitar
Soon you'll drive a car
Baby you'll go far
You're gonna be a star.

A whole other world is just
Behind the door
Get any girl you want
And she will beg for more
People think you're cool
They never did before
That's what you've been searching for.

You're gonna be a star
Oh, yes you are
You play your cheap guitar
Soon you'll drive a car
Baby you'll go far
You're gonna be a star.

The music continues. SHIRLY speaks to the audience.

SHIRLY: Everyone looks older, but if you look closely you can see
that they're the same kids who danced to the music fifteen years
ago when they were young and scared and the music was the
most important thing in their lives.

The band sings "King of Friday Night":

We may grow old and we may grow cold
And scared and stiff and fat
We may turn thirty with minds so dirty
That we don't know where it's at.
We don't care 'cause we once was there
And even though it may sound trite
We'll be young again when we remember when
We were the King of Friday Night.

Life's so hard, Daddy told me
And I know my daddy thought he was right
Life's so hard, Daddy told me
But he weren't the King of Friday
Weren't the King of Friday
Weren't the King of Friday Night.

Ooo we're the King of Friday Night
The King of Friday Night
Ooo we're the King of Friday Night
The king of Friday Night
Ooo we're the King of Friday Night
The King of Friday Night.

The music continues. SHIRLY speaks to the audience:

SHIRLY: But do you know what the really amazing thing is? I look
down into the crowd, and I look at the Monarchs, and everyone
is smiling. Everyone is happy. No one can think of a finer place
to be, than an ordinary town called Mushaboom, on a Friday
night.

The band plays "Rock and Roll":

When you're in the pit
And you're full of shit
And you don't know what to do
When you can't relate
'Cause you're two years late
And you missed your rendezvous.

When your mind is dumb
And your heart is numb
And you're fallin' down the hole
When it's time to face the music
You better rock
You better roll.

You better rock, you better roll
When the situation's out of control
When the situation's out of control
You better rock
You better roll.

Stop playin' that waltz
'Cause it's got its faults
And it ain't so sweet no more
And your favourite rhumba
Is now a bumma
And they laughin' you off the floor.

Put last year's hit
In the garbage pit
'Cause the gold has turned to coal
When it's time to face the music
You better rock
You better roll.

You better rock
You better roll
When the situation's out of control
When the situation's out of control
You better rock
You better roll.

You better rock, you better roll
When the situation's out of control
You better rock, you better roll
When the situation's out of control.

The music stops.

PARKER: Thank you, ladies and gentlemen. On behalf of the
Monarchs I wanna thank you for makin' the first and last reunion
a big success. This will be your home waltz.

*The band put down their instruments and come downstage, holding
quarts of beer. They sing "Hello Tomorrow," which is a toast, to piano
accompaniment:*

Here's to the beers I haven't drunk yet
And here's to all the women I ain't laid
Here's to the thoughts I haven't thunk yet
Here's to all the money I ain't made.

Here's to the priests who ain't forgiven
And all the rich who are feelin' poor
Here's to the lives that ain't been livin'
Here's to those who don't know much for sure.

Hello tomorrow
Hell with yesterday
Hello tomorrow
Just won't go away
Still your fears a few more years
You'll make it anyway
Hello tomorrow
Hell with yesterday.

The band hums accompaniment to SCREAMIN' JOHN, who sings a verse:

Here's to the hearts that ain't been broken
And all the dreams that ain't been satisfied
Here's to the lies that ain't been spoken
Here's to all the love that hasn't died.

Everybody sings:

Here's to everyone who ain't gone crazy
Here's to everyone who's still got ears
Here's to your eyes, and what they may see
Here's to all the days and all the years.

Hello tomorrow
Hell with yesterday
Hello tomorrow
Just won't go away
Still your fears a few more years
You'll make it anyway
Hello tomorrow
Hell with yesterday.

Curtain.

Don Messer's Jubilee

Preface

When I play on my fiddle in Doony
Folk dance like a wave of the sea.

—William Butler Yeats

The danger comes when they start calling you a writer. That's when the offers of commissions start to roll in. That's when the producers, entrepreneurs and arts administrators seek to use your skills to express their theories.

Any artist in Canada contends with powerful, energetic people who believe themselves to be creative visionaries who would astonish the world, were it not for one missing detail: Talent, for which they substitute Theory.

This mysterious thing called Talent, this ineffable spark, has by some quirk of nature been vested willy-nilly in overgrown children who don't know how to put it to use, who don't know what "sells." To ensure that talent is not squandered on the whims of artists, the producer, entrepreneur or arts administrator provides guidance: filters out the "bad" ideas, introduces and encourages the "good" ideas, according to whatever theory they believe, in what might be termed the Weed And Feed approach to human creativity.

Since *Billy Bishop Goes to War*, I have been offered the opportunity to write about William Lyon Mackenzie King, Tommy Douglas, Brother Twelve, Stan Rogers, William Duncan of Metlacatlan, Gweneth Lloyd, Stompin' Tom Connors and the Famous People Players. Had I any time or enrgy left, I could have written musical versions of *Lysistrata*, *The Orestia*, all of Shakespeare's comedies and Whiting's *The Devils*. My chances of securing a production of whatever it is I happen to be writing at the time, however, have not improved all that much.

This is not to ridicule or to condemn these proposals, most of which are perfectly sound subjects for musicals. But, taken together, they point out what seems to be an occupational hazard: in this technological age of specialization, it is common to think of a writer as a typist who specializes in storytelling, with the result being a lot of theoretically fine but mediocre work that lacks only passion, belief and a deep need to exist.

I encourage all writers who are receiving offers of commissions to stop and think about the uncertainties of life, and to be very careful of how much time you spend fluffing up the pillow. That's what I did when Tom Kerr of the Neptune Theatre in Halifax asked me if I might be interested in writing a musical about Don Messer, the taciturn Maritime fiddler who had an astonishing following across Canada for sixty years, until the cancellation of his television show in 1969 and his death a few years later.

Kerr had just made a success of my first, possibly only, non-musical, a thriller-farce entitled *Better Watch Out, You Better Not Die*, in a production that was better than the script, and I am always pathetically grateful to anyone who takes a chance on me. Although my reflexive response was "I don't do commisssions," I replied that I would think about it. Like most Canadians, I don't like to give an absolute yes or no to anything. It's something we have in common with the Japanese.

The strange thing is that I actually did think about it, for nearly a year; I even found myself scribbling notes. But when Kerr telephoned from time to time I remained coy, because I don't do commissions. Sometimes I behave like a character out of Dickens.

My initial reaction to the memory of Don Messer was a kind of nauseous ennui that many Canadians experience when the words "Canadian" and "culture" appear in the same sentence, a sensation that could easily be confused with hatred, a mild version of the ingrained revulsion a member of the Hitler Jugend must have felt for Jews, except in my own case the objects of my loathing were my own people, my own culture, elements of myself.

I remember my grandfather, listening to Don Messer and his Islanders on the floor radio in the overheated kitchen of the farmhouse with the rubber tray of boots at the door, lying on the battered chaise longue beside the wood-burning stove. I can't have been more than three, but if you put on a Don Messer record I can recall what combination of rings on the party line meant that the phone was for us, and what the well water tasted like. At other times I can remember kneeling on my hands and knees in front of the black-and-white Phillips television set from R.H. Jones Hardware, my father telling me to, "Be quiet, can't you be quiet, so a person can listen to something?" as the two generations behind me huddled before the plain, plump female singer and the slightly apoplectic, giant tenor with the pencil moustache, and listened to "Bless This House."

The tenor was Charlie Chamberlain, who lived in Truro for a while and who could be seen in the company of a bootlegger who, they say, had once amassed a fortune, but now had nothing but a rusted-out Cadillac and a dog with gold teeth.

By the time I was a teenager playing with rock and roll bands, Don Messer had become an object of shame. If we were going to have roots, we wanted them to be represented by craggy blues singers from Detroit, not by a nervous little fiddler from Tweedside. To their audiences, both Don Messer and Howlin' Wolf were cultural representatives from one generation to the next, and their music gave form to a sense of who they were and where they came from. And I am certain there were young Detroit blacks who despised the blues singer for keeping alive a past that they wanted no part of. Traditional music has been in a steep decline ever since the Beatles, and in a few years everyone on earth will be humming the same multinationally-promoted recording. Here in Canada, the worldwide current and our ingrained colonial assumptions joined forces, and our rejection of our roots took on a peculiar ferocity. The Islanders were to us what the Rolling Stones were to our parents: we wanted Messer annihilated, for all traces of that centuries-old music to be wiped from the face of the earth. We wanted the Global Village, not the Maritime variety, and in this we were joined by the perennial Canadian Aesthetes, those among us who always want Canadian culture to grow along the lines of some other culture they admire. Together we made a powerful lobby, and we won.

Ever with a moist finger to the prevailing wind, our national broadcasting system sent Messer a telegram one spring telling him not to return in the fall, thank you, and good luck in the future. After half a century of service, with neither ceremony nor pension, the band was replaced by something more "youth-oriented."

It's easy to blame the institution for this. Corporations seldom take responsibility for the ill that they do, so they make a nice, big target. But the fact is, most Canadians applauded the decision as an indication that Canada had come of age, had rejected its corny rural underpinnings in favour of something more urban, more connected with current international trends, more "world-class."

By now I had a personal connection to a good story, full of irony and pathos. It even had an "international dimension": African children are embarrassed to perform their native dances because they want to look like American pop stars. Each year there are fewer languages in the world. One of China's most popular singers is someone named Barbra Streisand, and surely we are not so naive as to believe that this will result in world harmony: people who are alike do not necessarily get along. We are all caught in a wave of homogenization: don't you worry from time to time that the world is becoming a less interesting place? Perhaps the worst thing about colonialism is that it is so boring.

I was still not making any promises to Neptune, but I did start writing now and again. From the beginning my purpose was therapeutic: I wanted to love the music of my ancestors, not to hate it, and what emerged was a sort of musical fan letter to an extinct group of musicians.

I screened videotapes of their old television program, and it became immediately evident that the format had never changed in fifteen years. The up-tempo fiddle tune, the romantic ballad, the square dance piece, the sacred music duet, all occurred at precisely the same moment in the show. That show was like a monument. Maybe I could create an easy-to-rehearse variety show that, for all its naive simplicity, had more than one level of meaning. Maybe I could communicate the charm of the subject while maintaining a degree of parody: I didn't want to become too pious, to take these characters more seriously than they took themselves.

Most important, I had a form that my audience would find more appropriate to the subject than the traditional European play structures.

With the character of Don Messer himself I was in a dilemma, for Messer was not a "personality" in the U.S. show business sense.

In fact he was just the opposite: painfully shy, he was seldom able to complete a sentence in public, and rarely said a word on television. Yet he was the centre of it all, and the band died with him: the empty centre without which everything falls apart. But how do you present that onstage, a medium which depends entirely on the spoken word? What do you do when your most important character can neither speak nor sing?

My solution was not to have him onstage at all, in the sense of having an actor impersonate him, but to have a representation of him present at all times, to maintain him as a ghost, a silent presence against which we were to hold our imperfect portrait of the band, the time and the music. This minor bit of surrealism would enable me to stray from a strict impersonation of his music: like all composers, I enjoy writing certain things and I do not enjoy others. Don Messer was going to have to make room for me, too, which didn't involve taking as much licence as you might think, for his sound was always a hybrid of whatever dances people were doing at the time. Any Canadian dance band in the 1930s was required to play both square and round dances, and to feature both old-time and big band instruments. No musician likes to sit out numbers, so it was inevitable that the clarinet played in the old-time numbers and the fiddles participated in the current hits, the result being a gloriously un-selfconscious intermarriage of styles: Celtic, oldtime, big band, Dixieland and hot jazz.

As long as I didn't write rock and roll, I had my pick of styles, but it would all have to seem plausible coming from a combination of instruments similar to the Islanders'. So I drew on all the styles I had tried out before *Rock and Roll*, leaned on one or the other according to subject matter, and united them by writing melodies similar to the Presbyterian hymns we sang every Sunday when I was a child: scale-based Celtic melodies that would make perfect sense sung without accompaniment.

In this I took a step forward: instead of referring directly to one popular musical form or the other, in *Don Messer's Jubilee* I wrote tunes that seldom referred directly to Messer's music but rather attemped to evoke the same effect in a contemporary audience. I couldn't simply assume that my audience liked the kind of music I was talking about, the way I could with *18 Wheels* and *Rock and Roll*: in fact it was safe to assume that my audience had rejected that kind of music a long time ago. My music in *Don Messer's Jubilee* was going to have outside reinforcement.

After a rehearsal period that seemed to be over in a matter of hours (Tom Kerr directed: I certainly wasn't going to try to get a show together that fast), *Don Messer's Jubilee* opened on January 4, 1985. I used the title of the television show, intending it to have a slight double meaning; this caused confusion among citizens who were unaware that he had been dead for over a decade. When it comes to Canadian culture, news travels slowly.

Reaction to the show varied from generation to generation, from class to class, from an almost evangelical purge of nostalgia, to tepid curiosity, to outright disdain. There were reports of mild hallucinations in which people saw not the stage but a black-and-white television screen, and Jodie Friesen and Frank McKay were thought by many to be virtual clones of Marg Osborne and Charlie Chamberlain, when in fact the resemblance is very faint. Some relatives of Messer and Osborne complained about an insufficient use of Messer's own music, and about the implication in the script that Marg's marriage was, as Don Tremaine once put it, "for the birds." Some theatre people thought the dancing was too good to be realistic, and the Artistic Director of a major theatre sniffed that the whole thing "lacked cultural fibre."

Critics variously characterized the piece as "nostalgic," "nationalistic," "tragic," "bitter," "heartfelt," and "stompin'."

Toward the end of the show there is a song called "Never Trust a Corporation" that caused me some trouble. In fact, at one party, a local IBM Canada executive took me aside and warned me darkly that I was biting the hand that fed me. And I am told that some executives within the national broadcasting system took exception to the piece, in remarkable solidarity with a decision taken almost twenty years earlier. Canadians have a reputation for being hard on themselves, but in reality we are highly sensitive to specific criticism.

There were critics in the west who thought that *Don Messer's Jubilee* was a fine piece of work except for the fact that it should never have been written. One scribe went on to defend the cancellation of the show as the one correct decision the network ever made. Another suggested that, if I wanted to lament the loss of a piece of television entertainment, why couldn't it have been "Star Trek"? But I try to write for audiences, not critics, and in the case of *Don Messer's Jubilee* Canadian audiences were more than willing to meet me halfway, whether or not they agreed with my version of the story. Sitting amid an audience humming "Smile the While" with

Marg and Charlie, I must say I felt quite at home.

I remember attending a performance of *The Resistable Rise of Arturo Ui* at the Berliner Ensemble in East Berlin. The show was performed a few metres from the Berlin Wall; people who might well have seen the man himself were laughing at Hitler. I had a sense that these people were connected to each other in ways that I, a Canadian, would never know. I felt lonely and out of touch. Around that time I found myself singing Celtic folk songs with some Irishmen. I was asked to sing a Canadian song, I couldn't think of one, and it was embarrassing. In the U.S.A. it bothered me when the news that I was Canadian elicited a blank, plexiglass stare as though I had for no reason given my Social Insurance Number.

I always come back to Canada determined to find out where Canada is, where I am, which is mostly a matter of determining where it is not, tracing my own tracks in the snow.

I believe the trick to surviving as an artist is to dig out a place for yourself in society that makes sense to you. Nobody is going to give you one, and in the vacuum it is tempting to become somebody's employee, a hired articulator for somebody else's ideas. That job pays well but there are occupational hazards. When you stop articulating what you think, soon you stop noticing what you think and, eventually, even if you can remember what it was you wanted to say to people back then, the prospect of putting your own ideas to the test, on spec, becomes far too terrifying to be worth the trouble. In this manner the artist inadvertently changes occupations, loses his grip on his own life, and his actions cease to have any meaning.

But as for me, I'm too perplexed to stop now.

Don Messer's Jubilee was originally produced by Neptune Theatre on January 4, 1985, and on tour from October, 1985 to Spring, 1986. The production starred Frank McKay, Jodie Friesen, Bill Carr and the Celtic folk band, McGinty. On tour, the part of Rae Simmons was played by Jarri-Matti Jelppi. The production was directed by Tom Kerr, with musical direction by John Gray, choreography by Linda Elliott and sets, lights and costumes by Stephen Deganson. The dancers were Linda Elliott, Katheryn MacLellan, Roy Cameron and Bob Paisley. The production was stage managed by Donna MacLauren.

Don Messer's Jubilee

Characters

RAE SIMMONS, the announcer and clarinet player. He wears 1940s-style eyebrow glasses, a double-breasted suit with a country-and-western bow tie, a pencil moustache and thin hair combed straight back. He looks like a cross between a country-and-western musician and a big band leader, which is what he is. He carries a clarinet, which he plays, or pretends to play.

MARG OSBORNE, a plump woman with a wide, plain face who sings well and has a vulnerable, friendly, decent quality. She dresses as though on her way to church, and tends to stand in the choir position with hands joined in front of her waist.

CHARLIE CHAMBERLAIN, a huge man with a red face and a pencil moustache, he is ideally suited to the singing of Irish songs. He plays the guitar and sings in a lyrical, moving tenor. Occasionally he step-dances.

THE ISLANDERS, a band consisting of guitar, bass, two violins, piano, and drums. They perform individually as singers, and together in harmony, in a variety of Celtic styles with elements of hot jazz, swing and big band music as well. They occasionally speak in unison.

THE BUCHTA DANCERS, four dancers, two male and two female, who perform a number of energetic dance routines in an embellishment of the square dance style. In "The Corporation Reel" they perform with dummies making up the square.

There must always be a representation of Don Messer onstage, a little man with a fiddle, grinning uncertainly at the audience.

Songs

"The Music Made Them Free"   The Islanders

"The Fiddler"   The Islanders

"Goin' to the Barndance" (Intro)   Marg & Charlie

"Some Advice From Marg"   Marg Osborne

"The Ballad of Charlie Chamberlain"   The Islanders

"My Little Flower"   Charlie Chamberlain

"Duke"   Rae Simmons & the Company

"A Song for Canada"   Charlie, Marg & the Company

"Plain Girls in Love"   Marg Osborne

"The Music Made Them Free" (Reprise)   The Islanders

"The Fiddler" (Reprise)   The Islanders

"Goin' to the Barndance" (Full)   Marg, Charlie & the Islanders

"It's Been Going On for Years"   Marg & Charlie

"The Corporation Reel"   Rae, the Islanders
                                       & the Buchta Dancers

"Never Trust a Corporation"   The Company

"Payday Companions"   Charlie Chamberlain

"For How Long"   Marg & Charlie

"Everybody Has Their Jubilee" (Finale)   Marg, Charlie
                                            & the Company

"Smile the While"   Marg & Charlie

NOTE: All songs by John Gray *except* "Goin' to the Barndance," "Smile the While," and the traditional jigs, reels and strathspeys.

Onstage are representations of CHARLIE CHAMBERLAIN, MARG OSBORNE, DUKE NEILSON and RAE SIMMONS, taken when they were young and so was the band.

The Islanders enter, tune up, and get ready to play. The actors playing CHARLIE and MARG enter, out of costume, and speak to the band, privately, then exit.

The house lights go to half. RAE turns and notices the audience for the first time. He wanders to the lip of the stage, to have a good look.

RAE: Amazing. Amazing, folks, is the only word that can describe what I feel when I look out over this audience tonight. If you'd have told me this many people would be coming out for a live show nowadays, well let me tell you, you could knock me over with a feather. *to Islanders* Isn't that right, boys?

THE ISLANDERS: *in unison* Amazing, Rae!

RAE: You bet it's amazing! Don't you people realize "Knot's Landing" is on tonight? We didn't think *anyone* went out of the house when "Knot's Landing" was on, did we, boys?

THE ISLANDERS: *in unison* Sure didn't, Rae!

RAE: You're darned right we didn't, and don't you think we don't appreciate it, either! *alarmed* Oh. Oh, gee. Gosh, I hope you folks didn't come all the way out here thinking you were going to be on TV. I sure *hope* you didn't, because this isn't that sort of thing at all, you see, no, no. No, we've got no cameras, no recording equipment, and there will be no re-run, let me tell you. When the evening is over, it will *really* be over, isn't that right, boys?

THE ISLANDERS: *in unison* Sort of like life, Rae!

RAE: You got it, boys! Now, hit it!

The house lights go out and the stage lights come up. We see a slide of Scottish immigrants landing in Nova Scotia in the eighteenth and nineteenth centuries. The Islanders play a series of chords that recall bagpipes and Scottish ballads, underneath the following speech.

RAE: Folks, you know I may just be the wrong man for this job, because our story begins long before I knew Don, Marg and Charlie, in fact, if you want to be strict about it, our story really begins about two hundred years ago.

The Islanders sing "From Culloden":

From Culloden and the clearance
Imperial interference
They made their disappearance
They sought another chance
Through poverty, repression
Political oppression
Their valuable possession
Was their music and their dance.

The Islanders begin a strathspey on fiddle and guitar underneath the following speech. A strathspey is a slow dance, half the speed of a reel, which usually breaks into a reel at some point. The dancers appear. We see a slide of a young child holding a violin, together with a picture of a turn-of-the-century village.

RAE: When you wonder why a plain, shy little fellow like Don Messer became one of the greatest stars in Canadian history, you have to remember that to rural Canada before the War the local fiddler was like an occult medium, bringing them the last echo of the voices of ancestors long turned to dust in the earth. It was their means of bringing the Old Country along with them, don't you see, without the fiddler they were just a bunch of impoverished people hacking away at the soil and the sea. So when a little village like Tweedside found out that the Old Countries were at war, and that same year saw a five year-old pick up the fiddle, well, I wouldn't be the one to say which event had the more vivid significance.

By this time the Islanders have changed tempo, and the dancers are now dancing a reel. The Islanders sing:

In every village and every town
The people came from miles around
On foot and horse and carriage and sleigh
To hear the local fiddler play
And the fiddler played like a man possessed
A touch of heavenly music blessed
Voices over time and sea

Ghosts were playing the melody
And they danced and they danced 'til they could not stand
Through sickness, war and cropless land
By the fiddler's bow and the fiddler's hand
The music made them free
The music made them free.

The dancers finish the reel, then return to a strathspey, which is played underneath the following speech.

RAE: Yes folks, if you want to know what made Don Messer more popular than Perry Como, Hockey Night in Canada, and, yes indeed, even Ed Sullivan himself, you're going to have to reach way back and imagine a time when music really meant something to people; when people liked music and liked themselves at the same time don't you see; a time when a tweeter and a woofer meant a bird and a dog; a time when people listened to Canadian music, not Japanese sound equipment.

We see a slide of a pre-adolescent boy in turn-of-the-century costume, playing the violin, as the Islanders sing a waltz:

Imagine a crowd of four or five hundred
Dancing to the Harvey Quadrille
In the flicker of gaslight
They'll dance 'til tomorrow
'Til the long morning shadows come over the hill
'Til the long morning shadows come over the hill.

They're spinning around an eight-year-old boy
He stands on a soapbox, playing alone
Playing "Haste to the Wedding"
When they call out "faster"
He plays every tune that he's ever known
He plays every tune that he's ever known.

The slide of the young violinist is joined by a slide of a barndance, taken at the turn of the century.

The sweat's pouring from him
Mosquitoes are biting him
He thinks his poor arms might fall to the floor
Born on the farm
Born to play fiddle
He dares not stop while the farmers cry "more"
No, he dares not stop while the farmers cry "more."

Through year after year
Through changes in fashion
He played on demand, like that small boy before
He played with love
And he played with passion
He played 'til the crowd didn't want him no more
He played 'til the crowd didn't want him no more.

The Islanders' fiddler plays a solo. This is all quite gentle and with a sense of being far away. We see a series of slides depicting the war, the depression, the dust bowl, the bomb, and other conspicuously twentieth-century imagery.

RAE: If you really want to know what Don Messer meant to people, I'm afraid you're going to have to imagine some unpleasant things, too. Like some eighteen-year-old from Flin Flon, listening to Messer on the wireless in an Allied field hospital, trying to forget that half his leg is gone and his friends are too, trying to remember that he has a home. Or a family in Saskatchewan, huddled next to the tiny speaker listening to Messer through the crackle and the hiss, trying to forget that the crops are corpses in the wind, and the man from the Royal Bank of Canada is coming over. Imagine people in pain, clinging to jigs, reels and hornpipes two hundred or three hundred years old, like lucky charms through relentless change. If you folks can imagine something like that, you might understand something about Don Messer and his Islanders.

The Islanders sing:

Bewildering changes, foreign illusions
It's a wonder a man can remember his name
Familiar faces, rest from confusion
Give thanks for some things that still stay the same
Give thanks for some things that still stay the same.

The music stops. RAE speaks to the audience. A representation of Don Messer is onstage, looking down at him. RAE refers to the actual names of performers in this speech, which should of course be replaced by whoever is in the cast.

RAE:
So, folks, suspend those questions
This isn't what you'd think
Jody won't look quite like Marg

And Frank won't smoke or drink
Just like Don, they're dead and gone
And we can't bring that back
But the spirit can make up for
The reality we lack
Like the spirit can give meaning to
A world that's on the move
Don, if you're up there watching
We hope that you approve.

With a flourish, RAE adjusts his glasses, picks up his clarinet, and delivers the characteristic announcement that opened every television show. From now on, RAE will assume his role as a 1950s announcer in the current style, and as such he is doubly anachronistic, being a figure of the 1950s and the 1940s at the same time.

RAE: And now, from Halifax, Nova Scotia and from coast to coast, it's the down-East music of Don Messer and his Islanders!

The Islanders break into the traditional "Fireman's Reel," which becomes the band's signature tune, "Goin' to the Barndance." Lights come up full, as CHARLIE and MARG enter amid the dancers, in a characteristic bit of choreography, then sing in harmony:

Got my dancin' boots on
Got my Sunday best
Goin' to the barndance tonight
Now dosey-do and balance
And swing 'em off their feet
Dancin' to the Islanders tonight.

The "Fireman's Reel" continues. RAE speaks over the music, as the announcer. This should be spoken as fast as possible and with breathless excitement.

RAE: Yes folks, we've got a great show lined up for you tonight, with Marg Osborne, Charlie Chamberlain, the Buchta Dancers and all the gang just itching to give you a little dose of something to chase away all those twentieth-century blues, with the old-time songs, the old-time stories and, yes, even some of the old-time dancing too, and let me tell you every word of it is about us, about Don Messer and his Islanders, so we've got a pretty good idea that by the time this is all over you folks are going to know us pretty well. And now without further ado, let's get on with the show!

CHARLIE and MARG emerge from the dancers to sing a reprise:

> Got my dancin' boots on
> Got my Sunday best
> Goin' to the barndance tonight
> Now dosey-so and balance
> And swing 'em off their feet
> Dancin' to the Islanders tonight.

The Islanders play one more verse of the "Fireman's Reel" and, with a flourish of choreography, the opening number comes to an end. RAE briskly steps up to the microphone, clarinet in hand.

RAE: And now to get things underway, let's listen to our own Marg Osborne, The Girl from the Singing Hills, the one person in the band we all knew the least about, except to say that she's just about the nicest person ever to walk the face of the earth! Ladies and gentlemen, here's Marg to sing one of the old favourites, "Some Advice From Marg"!

The Islanders play an introduction, as MARG steps modestly to the microphone to sing "Some Advice From Marg," a two-step with elements of hot jazz. She stands in the choir girl pose with hands joined in front of her waist and one foot slightly in front of the other, which is supposed to make legs appear more slim.

> When I was just a little girl
> My mother said don't try
> She said don't make a big mistake
> Don't set your sights too high
> Talent, personality will never stand the test
> Lose some weight, get your teeth straight
> And just hope for the best.

> She said maybe then some older men
> Who're somewhat well-to-do
> Will hear you singing sweetly, and
> Will take a shine to you
> Know what you're worth, be down-to-earth
> Be glad for what you get
> Don't talk too loud, avoid the clouds
> And there's hope for you yet.

> But I said . . .

There is an abrupt lighting change as MARG sings the chorus, which is almost burlesque, with Ethel Merman overtones. MARG breaks out of her characteristic pose with gestures in keeping with her inner self.

Maybe rats long to be cats
And horses want to fly
Maybe cats are tigers
When you look them in the eye
Stranger things have happened
In this world so far
Never give up hope, girls
Even I became a star.

The lighting becomes normal again and MARG goes back to her characteristic pose, slightly embarrassed. The Islanders play a hot jazz solo as she speaks. CHARLIE, who is playing guitar with the band, listens carefully.

MARG: Well in 1947, when Mr. Messer asked me to join his band, I suppose you could say I wasn't the most glamorous thing in the world.

CHARLIE: Nobody would disagree with you on *that*, Marg.

The Islanders snicker.

MARG: You be quiet, Charlie. In fact, my teeth were crooked, I had to get them fixed to appear on television, I was a *little* overweight, and I was very shy. But do you know what Mr. Messer said? He said, "Marg, you have the sweetest voice in the Maritimes, and if the men are looking for Ava Gardner, the women are looking for someone like themselves who can sing for them, and Marg, I think you're just the girl!"

MARG sings:

Mother shook her head so sadly
The way Maritimers do
Know your place and hide your face
Ambition is taboo
The Lord will teach the over-reacher
Lessons cruel but true
Throw away those dreams, ambitious schemes
Or there's no hope for you.

But I said . . .

172

Lights change. MARG breaks free again.

Is there a Berkeley Square
Is there a place called France
Why not a place where every race
Is free to sing and dance
Stranger things have happened
In this old world, so far
Never give up hope, girls
Even I became a star.

MARG assumes her normal pose again as the Islanders play an instrumental break. She speaks to the audience:

MARG: Well, with the radio show and the tours and then the television the letters just poured in, hundreds of them every week from women saying, "Marg, you're just like me, don't ever change!" And you know, I blush to say it, but every week I get at least one marriage proposal, imagine that!

CHARLIE: Difficult to imagine that, Marg.

The Islanders snicker.

MARG: You stop that, Charlie.

She sings:

The maiden aunts who say you can't
Have forgotten how to dream
Won't let you grow, they'll keep you low
And break your self-esteem
Don't underrate what's on your plate
It may be caviar
And never give up hope, girls
Even I became a star.

Maybe . . .

MARG breaks free again for a chorus and finale.

Someday we'll learn that maybe worms
Are snakes that didn't try
Maybe hens are eagles
Who never sought to fly
Stranger things have happened
In this old world, so far
Never give up hope, girls
Even I became a star.

Never give up hope, girls
Never give up hope, girls
Never give up hope, girls
Even I became a star.

The song ends with a flourish. MARG bows modestly and exits, as RAE steps up to the microphone with his clarinet, leading the audience in applause.

RAE: Now wasn't that just lovely, folks? Marg will be back in a while, but right now it looks like the Islanders have cooked up something special concerning someone everyone knows real well, some might say all *too* well. Here's the Islanders to give us "The Ballad of Charlie Chamberlain."

The Islanders step forward to play and sing "The Ballad of Charlie Chamberlain," with RAE narrating during the instrumental passages. This number is a Celtic ballad featuring a high tenor and harmony, with instrumental passages played by a synthesizer programmed to sound like Irish bagpipes.

It could make you cry, to hear him sing
Songs of old emotion . . .
A voice like a New Brunswick spring
A thirst to drown the ocean.

We see a slide of World War I troop trains, packed with young soldiers.

In Bathurst the trains stop
Full of uniformed young men
All to fight the Great War
Fewer to come back again
Already they are homesick
For the village and the farm
Shoulders used to slinging pitchforks
Not the punch of firearms
The war won't end by Christmas
Who knows when it will end
Those among the lucky
Will come back without a friend
But down beside the tracks
Is a curly-haired young boy
Singing old familiar tunes
In threadbare corduroy
Scenes of homes they left

174

And the girls they should be kissing
Gathering pennies thrown by
The future dead and missing.

It could make you cry to hear him sing
Songs of old emotion . . .
A voice like a New Brunswick spring
A thirst to drown the ocean.

Instrumental break. RAE speaks over the music, with slides of CHARLIE at various ages and in various costumes.

RAE: Charlie came right out of the New Brunswick woods. All his life he wore lumberjack clothes, long johns and old corduroy slippers. He had to have his shirts specially made because he wore a size 21 collar. Smoked incessantly, striking wooden matches with his thumbnail, and he loved to drink, always out of mickeys, never quarts, so he could hide it in his back pocket if he had to. He was always broke spending money on his friends, and every summer he had to pump gas in Timberlee or St. Margaret's Bay. Just about everyone has an uncle like Charlie, if they're lucky.

We see slides of early twentieth-century lumberjacks. The Islanders sing:

In the New Brunswick bush
Around a dying fire
Against the black flies and the chill
Men sit lonely and tired
Facing injury
For fifty cents a day
When they're broken for the work
Like old tools thrown away
He strums an old guitar
And he dances gracefully
Smiling in the firelight
Weathered as the trees
Some beat nails on horseshoes
Others simply hum along
Lost in awakened pleasures
As they listen to his song
He's a big lumberjack
With an Irish voice so clear
A brother to protect them
In their loneliness and fear.

It would make you cry to hear him sing
Songs of old emotion
A voice like a New Brunswick spring
A thirst to drown the ocean.

Instrumental break. RAE speaks over the music.

RAE: Charlie was a gentleman, the self-appointed protector of all
the girls on tour: musicians are a lecherous bunch of buggers,
you know. He was crazy about his wife, a French lady named
Lydia from Buldoon, out of the woods like himself and nearly
as big as him, too. He was always trying to buy the girls' ear-
rings, to give to Lydia.

The Islanders sing:

Thirty-five years later
Charlie's still working-class
In winter he's a star
In summer he pumps gas
Loves a hard-luck story
Charlie's always nearly broke
But there's a pint for any man
Who can tell a decent joke

Plaid shirt and battered slippers
Chain-smoking cigarettes
The good he sings about
The bad he just forgets
A man without ambition
He means nobody harm
A ringing baritone
A ton of Irish charm
A figure from the past
In this time of buy and sell
Charlie was just Charlie
Would that we could do so well.

It could make you cry to hear him sing
Songs of old emotion
A voice like a New Brunswick spring
A thirst to drown the ocean
It could make you cry.

End song. The Islanders return to their places and prepare to accompany CHARLIE, as RAE announces:

RAE: And now here's the man himself, Charlie Chamberlain, to sing one of my favourites, "My Little Flower"!

The Islanders play an introduction to a jig. CHARLIE enters with a great deal of bluster and sings "My Little Flower," an Irish music hall turn:

Oh my little flower, ma belle amour
No less now that she's quite mature
She gives me as much as I can endure
I'd certainly not ask for more.

Oh my little flower, my little 'tit belle
She may possibly kill me, but time will tell
She's a très formidable mademoiselle
I'd certainly not ask for more.

She is my little flower
Her skin is soft and white
But of course there was the difficulty
Late the other night . . .

The music becomes mock mysterioso. CHARLIE performs a little mime and sings:

I was quiet as a mouse
When I got back to the house
Somewhat under the weather
She was waiting by the fridge
When I got a bever-edge
You could have knocked me over with a feather
Then the dishes start to fly
Sharp was my darling's eye
One by one they cracked upon my head, then
Next came the forks and spoons
We bought on our honeymoon
It's a wonder that I weren't knocked dead, then
And when I hit the tile
I thought with a smile
It must have been the lateness of the hour
Tomorrow, if I rise
I must apologize
To my little flower.

The Islanders play a jig. CHARLIE dances for eight bars, then sings:

Oh my little flower, she's six foot three
Two hundred pounds are enough for me
She's a woman of scope and complexity
I'd certainly not ask for more.

Yes, my little flower, she's quite a sight
Her left is good, but beware her right
She's a woman of courage and appetite
I'd certainly not ask for more.

She is my little flower
She is my belle amour
But of course there was the trouble
On the Massey-Ferguson tour . . .

The music becomes mysterioso again. CHARLIE performs a little mime, then sings:

There was some rum in the trunk
And I got a little drunk
In the car on the way to Bathurst
We had a little fight
It was somewhat impolite
She mentioned some names and I cursed
No danger did I fear
She needed both hands to steer
I sat back, thinking what the heck, when
She let out an awful roar
And she kicked me out the door
I very nearly broke my neck then
And the one thing I knowed
As I bounced down the road
At fifty miles an hour
I'll be in the back seat
When next I drive down the street
With my little flower.

Oh my little flower, my little 'tit belle
My little smoked herring, my mackerel
She may possibly kill me, but time will tell
I'd certainly not ask for more.

Yes, my little flower, she's so petite
Her dress is chic and her smile is sweet
Whether love or war I admit defeat
I'd certainly not ask for more, no
I'd certainly not ask for more, no
I'd certainly not
Certainly not
Certainly not ask for more.

The song ends with a flourish, and CHARLIE bows and exits, with RAE leading the applause.

RAE: What did I tell you? Wasn't that fun? Well you know, Folks, Don Messer never was much of a talker, even his own family never really knew much about him, felt uncomfortable meeting people and talking with people, and he'd often sneak out of the hall during the home waltz so he wouldn't have to face so many strangers. Odd for a bandleader, but fortunately for Don he had his alter ego right there in the band playing bass.

We see a slide of DUKE NEILSON, in his prime.

Duke Neilson! The greatest bullshitter of them all, if you'll pardon my French.

The Islanders play the intro to "The Duke Neilson Two-Step," which is played in conjunction with an old-time reel. The entire cast comes onstage for this number as we see various slides of Duke Neilson, the New Brunswick Lumberjacks, and Backwoods Breakdown, as Don Messer looks on.

"The Duke Neilson Two-Step" is a hot jazz two-step featuring fiddle, bass and guitar in a style reminiscent of 1930s hot jazz.

RAE: And now, here's the whole gang to tell you all about the Duke and the early days of the band! Take it away, boys!

ALL: *singing*
Duke, Duke where are you now we need you
The country is as boring as a plough, now
Duke, Duke where are you now we need you
Duke, come out and take a bow.

RAE:

Well his father played for John Philip Sousa
His mother for the Woodstock Sally Ann
They got married, had a son
Banjo pick was on his thumb

ALL:

When he could walk he joined the band.

Minor key.

RAE:

But who knows what the future hides
What fate and accident decide
Father died, Mom went away
The orphanage walls were grey
Well, the Duke thought the orphanage wasn't quite his style
The music out of tune, the singers didn't smile
So one night he broke out clean
Joined the Navy, made the scene
But playin' bugle weren't his dream

ALL:

Marching single file.

RAE:

So the Duke quit the Navy, joined the circus
Drum-beater, fire-eater, banjo-player, dragon-slayer
Bear-fighter exciter, razorback, maniac
Nothin' that old Duke couldn't do, no, no, no

ALL:

Nothin' that old Duke couldn't do.

The Islanders break into a reel. RAE speaks over the music in the style of a carnival barker. The dancers do a routine.

RAE: Well that's when Don Messer ran into the Duke, a nineteen-year-old hotshot carney with a fast mouth and a flashy style. He liked the Duke right away because the Duke was everything Don wasn't, so Don and Duke formed the Backwoods Trio with Charlie Chamberlain, the Singing Lumberjack. Don handed the Duke a broken-down old bull fiddle and told him he was the bass player. The Duke fixed the thing in two days. Learned how to play it in one.

The reel comes to an abrupt end, to be replaced by the two-step as RAE sings:

Together they played the gaslight circuit
Bass strapped on the Model A
They got on radio, St. John, CFBO

ALL:
Drinkin', laughin' all the way.

The Islanders switch to the reel again. Another dance routine.

MARG: I have no idea what people see to admire in a bunch of drunken louts.

CHARLIE: Oh Marg, would you lighten up, for heaven's sake? *to audience* In Woodstock they danced so hard to "Flop-Eared Mule" and "Little Burnt Potato" that the verandah collapsed. When we played "Jimmy's Favourite Pig" in Kennotcook, two of the men had to stop dancing and hold up the roof. In Hopewell, the pillars collapsed during "Spud Island Breakdown." The people just threw them out the window and kept right on dancing. We had quite an effect on the architecture of the province.

CHARLIE does a little dance as the reel finishes and is replaced by the two-step again.

RAE:
Well Don kept the people's feet dancing
And Duke was the magician at the fair
Him and Charlie raising hell
With a dirty joke to tell

ALL:
In his spare time he wrestled bears.

The two-step continues.

RAE: By the late thirties they were the New Brunswick Lumberjacks, eighteen pieces and hot as hell, second only to George Wade and his Cornhuskers, which will give you folks some idea of just how hot they were. They were touring right down to New York City, even played for FDR himself. Once Eddie Cantor saw Charlie and tried to get him to go to Hollywood as a singing cowboy, but Charlie was having too much fun for all that American stuff.

CHARLIE: Got a letter from . . . Marg, what was that fellow's name in the Adirondack Mountains?

MARG: Willett Randall.

CHARLIE: Willett Randall, that's right, Marg. Well old Willett wrote: "The last time you played Redwing, our boys stomped the pine knots clear through the men's room floor!"

RAE: *singing*
Well they played from New York to Dawson City
Drivin' on dirt roads all the way
In 1930s cars, just like rock and roll stars

ALL:
Drinkin', laughin' all the way.

Minor key.

RAE: Then the depression hit the New Brunswick Lumberjacks like a bad epidemic of the flu, and one by one musicians dropped off until it was just Don, Charlie and Duke again, so they called themselves Backwoods Breakdown. With the St. John radio show second only to the Happy Gang and with five dollars a night on the barndance circuit they got by, but the Duke started thinkin' the Maritimes weren't big enough for him. You hear that sort of thing even today, I understand.

The Islanders break into the reel again. The dancers do a routine.

CHARLIE: When we played Mulgrave, there were no hotels then so the people put us up for the night, and the Duke ends up with this old Scottish spinster, you know the type, and in appreciation for her hospitality he does some card tricks and eats some fire. Whether it was the card tricks or the fire we don't know but suddenly the woman screams: "The devil is in this house! The devil is in this house!", and she goes after the Duke with a hatchet! Not long after that, the Duke quit the band.

The Islanders play the two-step again. RAE sings.

RAE:
Well the Duke made up his mind to hit the big time
Maybe Montreal would offer something new
Benny Goodman heard him play
He was heard to say

ALL:
Nothin' that old Duke can't do.

Minor key.

RAE:
But the Duke thought Benny Goodman wasn't quite his style
Jazz was hot but he was missin' Don and Charlie all the while
They say that it's a fact
Maritimers all come back
Duke said, "My bags are packed"
Don won't you . . .

ALL:
Take me back, I'll make you smile.

The Islanders break into the reel, while the dancers perform another routine.

RAE: Now by this time the CBC cancelled the radio show for reasons known only to themselves, not the last time you'll hear of that sort of thing, and Don and Charlie had hooked up with CFCY in Charlottetown, playing with a PEI group called The Islanders, including yours truly. Well I'll tell you, when the Duke showed up, Don was so happy to see him, I think I saw his expression change. Don said:

ALL:
Duke, Duke where are you now we need you
Without you I'm as boring as a plough, now
Duke, Duke where are you now we need you
Duke, come out and take a bow.

RAE: Well the Duke came back to stay, but a few years later the conductor of the Boston Pops came to PEI on vacation, and Mr. Fiedler was supposed to be at a tea party at CFCY, but he didn't show up. Turns out he and the Duke spent the day in the garage the Duke was living in at the time, and Fiedler offered him a job with the Boston Pops, a "chair" they call it. But the Duke said, "Thanks, Art. I'm sittin' pretty good right here!"

ALL:
Duke, Duke where are you now we need you
The country is as boring as a plough, now
Duke, Duke where are you now we need you
Duke, come out and take a bow.

Duke, Duke where are you now we need you
The country is as boring as a plough, now
Duke, Duke where are you now we need you
Duke come out and take a bow, yeah
Duke come out and take a bow, yeah
Duke come out and take a bow.

The Islanders play a reel finale. On the last two bars, the cast chants:

We don't care why, we don't care how
Duke come out and take a bow!

End song. Blackout.

We hear a tight, Scottish snare playing a march-like rhythm. We see a series of slides depicting Don Messer and his Islanders in various situations over the years, ending with their 1967 cross-Canada tour. MARG and CHARLIE sing "A Song for Canada," with the whole cast joining in on the chorus:

The land goes on forever
It just never seems to end
Without a single border to confine me
I can travel any distance
Anywhere I want to turn
If I want to I can leave it all behind me.

In the forest, on the prairie
On the road and on the rails
On the lakes and on the mountains and the sea
For some it's all for nothing
And for some it's all for sale
But Canada, you mean the world to me.

Oh it may be out of fashion
And sophisticates may scorn
But it's natural to care about
The land where you were born
Our outlook is divided
Our loyalties are torn
Could we spare a song for Canada, the homeland.

It's not as though we own it
We're just keepers of the land
And hungry mouths are waiting 'cross the sea

I fished in the Atlantic
I played music with a band
Helped a farmer clear a field among the trees.

We live peacefully together
That's the way we will survive
Don't have to kill each other to be free
You may mean something different
To every man alive
But Canada, you mean the world to me.

Oh it may be out of fashion
And sophisticates may scorn
But it's natural to care about
The land where you were born
Our outlook is divided
Our loyalties are torn
Could we spare a song for Canada, the homeland
Could we spare a song for Canada, the homeland
Could we spare a song for Canada, the homeland.

Fade to black.

Lights up, revealing MARG, standing beside a small table with a telephone. She dials the operator.

MARG: Hello? Operator? Yes, could you give me 429-7300 in Halifax, Nova Scotia, please? Yes, that's right. Thank you very much. *She waits for someone to answer.* Oh, come on. Please answer. Five rings, six rings, most people hang up by six but I'll give it two more, maybe you're in the yard, well, maybe just one more and then I'll . . . *to operator* Yes, Operator, I can hear that the party doesn't answer. I'll try again later, yes. Thank you very much.

She hangs up, but immediately dials the operator again.

Hello, Operator? Yes, could you give me 429-6619 in Halifax, Nova Scotia, please? Yes, that's right. Thank you very much, station-to-station would be fine. Goodness knows I wouldn't mind a wrong number at this point, just to . . . Hello? Joyce, is that you? It's Marg. Oh, Joyce, I'm sorry, is it that late, I keep forgetting about time zones and whether it's earlier or later back home, and anyway I wanted to hear someone's voice, I was beginning to think there'd been another Halifax explosion and everyone had . . . what? Speak up, Joyce, you sound like you're under water. Oh, we're in Winnipeg, at least I think we are, it's so hard to keep track any more, but three people froze last night on the way to the grocery, so we must be in Winnipeg. Oh, they're all at the tavern I suppose, except for Mr. Messer of course, even the girls are out from sheer boredom, it's like the flu. Charlie is frantic trying to round them up so he can go and get drunk with a clear conscience . . . what? Listen, Joyce, it's hard enough to hold your head up in this business without getting involved in that sort of thing. Joyce, the reason I phoned was I was wondering if you'd seen Carson, maybe there's something wrong with our phone but I can't seem to . . . what? Yes, it is lovely, isn't it, Carson always wanted a convertible and . . . oh. I see. Not in the yard. Three days, yes, I see. Well, Joyce, I know it's late, so I'm going to let you go now. Kenora tomorrow, at least we're going east. I'll talk to you soon. Joyce, please don't say anything. Thanks. 'Bye.

She hangs up. She picks up the telephone again and dials, as the Islanders play the introduction to "Plain Girls in Love." She thinks better of it, hangs up, and sings:

There's no hope for them
Lovers ignore them
The voice on the radio
Is their only friend
I know they're listening
This song is for them
Plain girls in love with
Conceited young men.

You said you loved me
You said I was pretty
A few extra pounds
Didn't matter at all
Oh how I loved you
You felt no pity
It must have amused you
When you saw me fall.

Nothing matters, but dazzle and glamour
Only the beautiful win in the end
If he asks you, think twice, love

That's the advice of
Plain girls in love with
Conceited young men.

You took my money
And my self-respect, too
Now I know that you'll hurt me
As much as you can
I can wait all night for you
I needn't expect you
A plain girl in love with
A conceited young man.

Nothing matters, but dazzle and glamour
Only the beautiful win in the end
If he asks you, think twice, love
That's the advice of
Plain girls in love with
Conceited young men.

*Instrumental break. MARG goes to the telephone, hesitates, then returns
to a microphone and sings:*

If I gave you a watch
A ring with a diamond
If I gave you a car
Could you love me tonight
Am I just a fool
You wasted some time on
Do you think you could love me
If I turned out the light.

Nothing matters, but dazzle and glamour
Only the beautiful win in the end
If he asks you, think twice, love
That's the advice of
Plain girls in love with
Conceited young men.

Plain girls in love with
Conceited
Young men.

End song. Fade to black.

Immediately, lights come up on the Islanders, who perform a reprise of the opening of the show:

From barndance to television
Log fire to nuclear fission
For a folk musician
Is a long, long way to go
He played with real emotion
With humour and devotion
As changeless as the ocean
His songs from long ago.

Tempo change: the Islanders play a reel, as CHARLIE enters briskly and speaks to the audience.

CHARLIE: Got a letter from some people in Vanguard, Saskatchewan about a crippled lady, a Mrs. K. Starr, who crawled on her hands and knees to a neighbour's house to watch Don Messer on TV. After a few weeks of this the neighbourhood couldn't take it any more, so they bought her a television set!

THE ISLANDERS: *singing*
In every village and every town
The people tuned in for miles around
On Westinghouse and RCA
To hear the local fiddler play
And the fiddler played like a man possessed
A touch of heavenly music blessed
Voices over time and sea
Ghosts were playing the melody
Familiar faces from the land
Someone not American
By the fiddler's bow and the fiddler's hand
The music made them free
The music made them free.

The Islanders play the reel as the dancers do a routine, then they sing:

Familiar faces from the land
Someone not American
By the fiddler's bow and the fiddler's hand
The music made them free.

The music becomes a strathspey as the DANCERS move offstage and RAE steps to the microphone and speaks to the audience.

RAE: Well you know, by the time Don Messer got on television he was a household word: not Messer himself, but his music, his sound, his people, and let me tell you folks, that was quite a feat, because hardly *any* radio show's *ever* made it on TV, because, you see, TV destroys people's mental privacy, the fantasy that plays in people's minds when they listen to the radio. But with Don Messer, what they saw was exactly what they imagined because, you see, he was the real thing.

The Islanders sing a reprise of the waltz from early in the show. At the same time we see a slide of the older Don Messer.

He's getting older
His heart gives him trouble
He never speaks, he's as shy as before
Born on the farm
Born to play fiddle
He cannot stop while the farmers cry "more"
No, he dares not stop while the farmers cry "more."

Through year after year
Through changes in fashion
He played on demand, like that small boy before
He played with love
And he played with passion
He played 'til the crowd didn't want him no more
He played 'til the crowd didn't want him no more.

Bewildering changes, foreign illusions
It's a wonder a man can remember his name
Familiar faces, rest from confusion
Give thanks for some things that still stay the same
Give thanks for some things that still stay . . .
The same.

The Islanders return to their places, still playing. As they do so, an old-fashioned television camera, manned by one of the dancers, dollies across the stage taking close-ups, then takes its place on the stage as the set becomes a naive 1950s-style television studio set.

A spotlight hits RAE with clarinet, and he announces:

RAE: And now from Halifax, Nova Scotia and from coast to coast, it's the down east music of Don Messer and his Islanders!

The Islanders break into the "Fireman's Reel," as the dancers do the opening routine. The costumes are a bit more elaborate, but the act is basically unchanged. MARG and CHARLIE take their places and sing "Goin' to the Barndance."

Got my dancin' boots on
Got my Sunday best
Goin' to the barndance tonight
Now dosey-do and balance
And swing 'em off their feet
Dancin' to the Islanders tonight.

MARG:
Talk about your struttin'
Just watch me put it on
I won't begin to get my wind
Until the break of dawn.

MARG & CHARLIE:
And we'll still be dancin'
When all the rest are gone
Goin' to the barndance tonight.

Hear that fiddle playin'

Fiddle break.

Goin' to the barndance tonight
Hear what that fiddle's sayin'

Fiddle break.

Goin' to the barndance tonight.

CHARLIE:
A little drink of cider
How good it makes you feel
Eight or nine and you will find
Blisters on your heels.

MARG & CHARLIE:
Got my dancin' boots on
Got my Sunday best
Goin' to the barndance tonight.

The Islanders reprise the "Fireman's Reel," and the song ends. In a flash, RAE steps to the microphone as announcer.

RAE: Well folks, when a band and a show have been in the public eye as long as we have, there's always more to it than *meets* the eye, and here to tell you all about it are our own Marg and Charlie with that old toe-tapper, "It's Been Going On for Years"!

The Islanders play the intro to a very up-tempo polka. CHARLIE and MARG sing a duet, "It's Been Going On for Years":

Stuck together
It's been going on for years
Singing old-time love songs
We try and look sincere
How this happened, we don't know
Why was never clear
Stuck together
It's been going on for years.

MARG:
Oh I don't know how I stand it
It's been going on so long
Singing duets with a slob
Whose breath is somewhat strong
Nicotine-stained fingers
With a pint of rum attached
I fear his breath will burst in flames
Whene'er he strikes a match.

CHARLIE:
Oh I don't know how I take it
She's much too pure for me
She wouldn't say shit if she stepped in it
Nobody's seen her knee
The professional virgin
She should be in a choir
If you gave her a wink she'd just turn pink
Then she would expire.

MARG & CHARLIE:
Stuck together
It's been going on for years
Singing old-time love songs
We try and look sincere
How this happened we don't know

Why was never clear
Stuck together
It's been going on for years.

The Islanders play an instrumental break, as CHARLIE and MARG snipe at one another.

MARG: Charlie, put out that cigarette, I can smell it, you're not supposed to smoke in the studio.

CHARLIE: Just listen to queasy womanhood here, next you'll want me wearin' after-shave.

MARG: During "Quiet Time" you spit on the floor and I nearly threw up on camera.

CHARLIE: You got no stomach at all, my girl, normally takes me two quarts of rum to do that.

MARG & CHARLIE:
Stuck together
It's been going on for years
Singing old-time love songs
We try and look sincere
How this happened we don't know
Why was never clear
Stuck together
It's been going on for years.

MARG:
I had a lovely dream last night
I dreamt he disappeared
No filthy joke, no haze of smoke
No three-day growth of beard
My dream became a nightmare
When the filthy man appeared
Drooling on my nice clean dress
And snapping my brassiere.

MARG & CHARLIE:
Stuck together
It's been going on for years
So fond of each other
That's how it must appear
How this happened we don't know

Why was never clear
Stuck together
It's been going on for years.

CHARLIE: You're slowin' down the tempo, Marg, at the rate you're goin' we'll not be out of here in time to trim the tree.

MARG & CHARLIE: *singing*
Are we doing penance
For some unremembered sin

CHARLIE:
Must I face her holy grace

MARG:
And I his stupid grin

MARG & CHARLIE:
Opposites do not attract
We have the proof right here
Would someone please explain
Why it's been going on for years . . .

CHARLIE:
Has there ever been a virgin queen
So holy and upright
Her fingernails are always clean
She's always so polite
I'd like to spike her tea with rum
I'd like to see her dance
On a table in the tavern
Wearing underwear from France.

MARG: Charlie! That's the most disgusting thing I've heard come out of your mouth yet, and I've heard some disgusting things!

MARG & CHARLIE: *singing*
Stuck together
It's been going on for years
We both remain about the same
Forever, it appears
How this happened we don't know
Why was never clear
Stuck together
It's been going on for years.

MARG:
  His personal habits
  I always will despise.

CHARLIE:
  If she's ever perspired
  I'd be very much surprised.

MARG & CHARLIE:
  But we seem to go together
  Like potato chips and beer
  Stuck together
  It's been going on for years
  Stuck together
  It's been going on for years
  Stuck together
  It's been going on for years.

*The song ends. CHARLIE and MARG bow, then leave together, as RAE
steps up to the microphone.*

RAE: Wasn't that great? I had a lot of fun, and I sure hope you
  folks did too, but I'm afraid we're going to have to forget about
  fun for a while, because we've come to that moment I know a
  lot of you folks have been waiting for, dreading, perhaps, and
  it's no fun for me either, because I was never one to speak ill
  of the dead. But we're going to have to talk about the Canadian
  Broadcasting Corporation. You see folks, even though we were
  the most popular show in the country for years, you've got to
  remember that to the CBC, popularity in itself is not as important as how that popularity reflects on, shall we say, the cosmetic
  ambitions of the people in charge. And a big corporation like the
  CBC is bound to contain a lot of . . . *He searches for le mot
  juste.* A lot of . . .
THE ISLANDERS: *in unison* Arseholes.
RAE: What was that, boys?
THE ISLANDERS: Arseholes, Rae!
RAE: *shocked* Now boys, boys, I won't be having language like
  that! *to a slide of Duke* Duke, are you puttin' these boys up to
  that? *to audience, ashamed* I'm sorry, folks, but what the boys
  were trying to tell you was that an organization like the CBC is
  bound to contain a lot of what you might call . . . culturally
  displaced persons.
THE ISLANDERS: Arseholes.

RAE: Now you cut that out! *to audience* Folks, let's just say that there are those among us whose feet may be in Canada but whose heads are . . .

THE ISLANDERS: Up their arseholes, har, har, har!

The Islanders are getting a bit rowdy. RAE refers to the slide of Duke again.

RAE: Duke, I'm not tellin' you again! *to the audience* Folks, it's pretty clear that the cancellation of Don Messer is still an emotional subject, and we don't want to get you folks all fired up. But fortunately we have the Buchta Dancers to tell us all about it. Ladies and Gentlemen, let's hear it for the Buchta Dancers and "The Corporation Reel"!

The four dancers enter, each with a partner which is a dummy on wheels. They will behave like a square dance set, except that the dummies can be mistreated more than human beings can. The following is choreographed square dancing, with the climax of each verse being a solid knife in the back of the dummies.

The Islanders play a medley of traditional reels, and RAE acts as caller for "The Corporation Reel":

Now honour your partner!
Honour your corner!

Well the year is nineteen fifty-six
Through Upper Canadian politics
We got TV, the CBC
To serve Canadian unity
Another crown corporation
That's the way to save the nation
Now all you bureaucrats have it made
Take a politician and promenade
Now you need some talent, just to start
Popular, not too much art
So everybody dosey-do
And search for talent on the radio
Join hands with that radio star
If it all works out, you'll both go far
But if those ratings should go slack
It's honour your partner
Stab 'em in the back!

Now circle high and circle low
Plunder regional radio
And gradually build up a stable
Of locals who seem to be able
To keep that network out of debt
Messer, Plouffe and Juliette
Now all join hands and have some fun
You just beat Ed Sullivan

But all you stars don't forget that
Your show belongs to the bureaucrats
For all your popularity
You're still corporate property
And good old popular tradition
Can't match corporate ambition
If you're not their style, you'll get the sack
It's honour your partner
Stab 'em in the back!

A la main left and dosey-do
Nineteen-sixties, here we go
Face the border, all join hands
Welcome those Americans
Texas star around the hall
All you bureaucrats start to drawl
Civil servants know the truth
Style's the thing and now it's youth
Now round the circle two by two
Grow your hair and sideburns too
Nehru jacket, chain of gold
Tired of the hand you hold
Change partners
But if your hair is short in back
It's honour your partner
Stab 'em in the back!

Now Maritimers all join hands
And imitate Ontarians
Promenade, two by two
We can be as cool as you
What are traditions all about
Grab your partner, throw them out
We wanna hear the Beatles sing

Messer is embarrassing
Now everybody all join hands
And imitate some foreign land
If worldliness is what they lack
It's honour your partner
Stab 'em in the back!

And should the future seem a trifle black
It's honour your partner, stab 'em in the back!

It's a way of life, that's a fact
Honour your partner, stab 'em in the back
Honour your partner, stab 'em in the back
Honour your partner, stab 'em in the back.

The music ends with a flourish, the dancers still enthusiastically stabbing their dummy "partners." Lights up. The dancers, mildly embarrassed, drag their partners offstage, as RAE approaches the microphone.

RAE: Yes, folks, in April of 1969 we got a telegram that the show was cancelled in favour of something more youth-oriented. And that was when the . . . when the . . .

THE ISLANDERS: *in unison* The shit hit the fan!

RAE: Oh, you should have seen the letters, the telegrams, the editorials all over the country, the questioning of Dr. Davidson in Parliament as to why they would butcher a cow that was still giving milk. But of course it was no use. In an unheard-of display of artistic integrity, the CBC held firm against the wishes of its audience, and we were off the air because we weren't . . . youth-oriented. And now for all you youths out there, who will some-day grow old, God willing, here's the whole gang with a little bit of career advice.

The cast comes onstage and sings "Never Trust a Corporation." There is a hot jazz-swing instrumental break in the middle, where the DANCERS perform a short routine.

Never trust a corporation
Corporations have no class
Their ethics are nonexistent
Their world outlook is crass
Don't join the careerists
Selling stock or pumping gas
Never trust a corporation
Corporations have no class.

Never, never trust the government
Don't trust a bureaucrat
Expanding their departments
The little autocrats
Shuffling their memos
Taking lunch and standing pat
Never trust the government
Don't trust a bureaucrat.

Oh, oh, oh
It's hard to adjust, who can you trust
In a world of frauds, and fakers
Stab from behind, rob you blind
From cradle to undertaker
How can you feel when nothing is real
When it's all merchandising
When everything you care about
Is a matter of advertising.

Never trust a hierarchy
Question every teacher
When stars appear, don't clap and cheer
Heckle from the bleachers
See the crook behind the king
The pimp behind the preacher
Never trust a hierarchy
Question every teacher.

No, never trust a leader
A John or Paul or Peter
The hungry-eyed succeeder
Flag-waver and drum-beater
The slimy bottom feeder
Materialistic cheater
Never trust, never trust
Never trust, never trust . . .
Don't trust any of them.

End song. Blackout.

Lights up to reveal CHARLIE, alone, sitting at a tavern table covered with a stained terry-cloth. He speaks to the empty chair opposite, to other men in the tavern who ignore him, and to himself.

CHARLIE: Oh 'tit Belle, my darlin' 'tit Belle, what's old Charlie gonna do now? We been thrown out, 'tit Belle, thrown out like broken old tools, and what're we gonna do now, eh, go back to the woods? Eh? Old Charlie can't go back to the woods no more, my little 'tit Belle: the muscles is soft from too much of the easy life, and the tubes is all burnt out from the cigarettes.

He looks up and recognizes someone.

George! George! Come over here and have a drink with old Charlie!

Pause.

George? Guess he didn't hear me. Old George is talkin' to some other fellas over there, known them for years. What're we gonna do my little 'tit Belle, old Charlie gonna move to Toronto? Sing at the Holiday Inn?

He sees another familiar face.

Allister! That you Allister? *Pause.* Guess he didn't hear me, either, old Charlie must be losin' his voice on top of everything else.

He takes a drink.

Thanks a lot, Charlie. Thanks a lot. That was a great forty years you gave us Charlie, now you just go home and take it easy, Charlie, you just go home.

Pause.

Go home, they said. Go home. Where's that, my little 'tit Belle? Where's that?

He stands up unsteadily but with dignity.

Boys, I'm gonna propose a little toast! Boys, do you hear me, a toast! *to himself* All right, then, I'm gonna propose a toast to myself.

Music: an Irish-style Celtic ballad accompanied by guitar, fiddle, and tin flute, called "Payday Companions." CHARLIE sings:

A small piece of paper twice a month came
Pay to the order of stood by my name
Pay to the order of one who depends
On payday companions and fair-weather friends.
On payday companions and fair-weather friends.

I swear that I meant to bring it right home
Darling, believe me I did
But just by old chance, I'd meet my old friends
Jimmy and Brian and Sid
To talk of the good times, to sing a few old rhymes
The way old companions will do
And when I awoke, they were gone, I was broke
And too drunk to come home to you, to you
Just too drunk to come home to you.

You see, Jimmy lost a leg in the war
Sid's been on pogey for years
And as Brian would say to me what's a friend for
If he can't buy an old friend a beer
Well over the years new old friends appeared
Just by chance, every payday they'd call
I was true to the end, to my fair-weather friends
And never thought of you at all, at all
Just never thought of you, at all.

So here's to my darlin', my little 'tit Belle
More than the others, you treated me well
Would that you had every cent I did spend
On payday companions and fair-weather friends
On payday companions and fair-weather friends.

Instrumental break. RAE enters and speaks over the music.

RAE: Now folks, don't let old Charlie fool you into thinking we're talking a lot of money here. Don made two hundred a week, Charlie a hundred and twenty-five, Marg a hundred and fifteen for the TV, and concerts? We made less than an unknown rock and roll band. Don was careful and frugal, and he never figured out what the band was worth.

CHARLIE: *singing*
Well it's funny how fast your fortunes can turn
They're as fickle as fair-weather friends

For the booze that I drank and the money I burned
You're all I have left in the end
Though all through the past I thought of you last
I still loved you more than I knew
And I swear that the day the Lord takes me away
This old heart will die loving you, just you
This old heart will die loving you.

So here's to my darlin' my little 'tit Belle
More than the others you treated me well
Would that you had every cent I did spend
On payday companions and fair-weather friends
On payday companions and fair-weather friends.

End song. The light on CHARLIE fades and RAE steps up to the microphone.

RAE: Well folks, we got kicked out, but the Islanders weren't finished yet. We got taken on by a private station in Hamilton, but the trouble was we were recording a show a day, rather than a show a week, for reasons of cost-effectiveness, don't you see. Well Charlie went first, heart attack, collapsed on the set. Then Don went, he'd had heart trouble for years, and that really was the end. Marg carried on as a solo act, then she had a heart attack too, five years to the day from Charlie. It might be putting things a bit strong, but you could say they all died of broken hearts. Which brings us to Quiet Time, folks, and here's our own Marg and Charlie to sing that old sacred music favourite, "For How Long."

CHARLIE and MARG enter and sing "For How Long," a Celtic hymn:

The evening sky grows dim and chill
I hear a church bell ring
The moon glows on the silent snow
A choir begins to sing
We're waiting for a time
When we will know where we belong
For how long
For how long.

The people bow their heads in prayer
A preacher's voice is heard
I know just what he's saying, though
I can't make out the words

We await a day when he will say
Just who was right or wrong
For how long
For how long.

For how long
For how long
If I only knew what is true
I know I could be strong
I wouldn't dream of asking you
What, or how, or why
Just how long
For how long.

Will I leave a memory
Behind me, when I'm gone
When darkness falls, who can recall
Just where the light has shone
The singer dies, as time goes by
But there remains the song
For how long
For how long.

For how long
For how long
If I only knew what is true
I know I could be strong
I wouldn't dream of asking you
What or how or why
Just how long
For how long.

The song ends. CHARLIE and MARG bow and exit, arm in arm. RAE steps to the microphone.

RAE: Wasn't that just lovely? Well, of course, no show would be complete without a word or two about the Islanders.

We see photographs of the Islanders one by one, as mentioned.

Well Cec McEachern on guitar, he became a file clerk, and Waldo Munro the piano player became a taxi driver in Halifax. Me, Rae Simmons, I became a maintenance man in a Charlottetown hotel. And Duke Neilson? Well, the Duke set up a bird sanctuary and game farm in Montague, PEI, you might say for endangered species like himself. Yes, like all life stories, this one has a sad ending, but we won't have all you folks feelin' down about this thing, and for everyone here who just might have a case of those life transition blues, Don, Marg, Charlie and the Islanders have a tune for you that just might do the trick. Here's the whole gang with that old barn-burner, "Everybody Has Their Jubilee"!

The entire cast enters and performs a medley of songs from the show, joined together by "Everybody Has Their Jubilee":

Everybody has their jubilee
Though sometimes the real things in life
Are difficult to see
Sometimes you're up, sometimes you're down
But it's all worth the fee
As long as
Everybody has their jubilee

CHARLIE:
I met a news announcer
His chin hung to the floor
He said I read the news each night
I just can't take no more
He said my wife, my kids, my life
Don't mean a thing to me
I said, Bud
You just might have missed your jubilee.

Everybody has their jubilee
Though sometimes the real things in life
Are difficult to see
Sometimes you're up, sometimes you're down
But it's all worth the fee
As long as
Everybody has their jubilee.

Key change. MARG and CHARLIE sing "Goin' to the Barndance."

Got my dancin' boots on
Got my Sunday best
Goin' to the barndance tonight
Now dosey-do and balance
And swing 'em off their feet
Dancin' to the Islanders tonight.

Instrumental "Fireman's Reel," with dancing. Key change. MARG reprises "Some Advice From Marg":

Maybe
Someday we'll learn that maybe worms
Are snakes that didn't try
Maybe hens are eagles
Who never sought to fly
Stranger things have happened
In this old world, so far
Never give up hope, girls
Even I became a star.

Key change. CHARLIE reprises "My Little Flower":

Oh, my little flower
She's six foot-three
Two hundred pounds
Are enough for me
She's a woman of scope
And complexity
I'd certainly not ask for more.

Oh, my little flower
My little 'tit Belle
My little smoked herring
My mackerel
I may not survive you
But time will tell
I'd certainly not ask for more, no
I'd certainly not ask for more, no
I'd certainly not
Certainly not
Certainly not ask for more.

Key change. CHARLIE and MARG reprise "It's Been Going On for Years":

Stuck together
It's been going on for years
We both remain about the same
Forever, it appears
How this happened we don't know

And why was never clear
Stuck together
It's been going on for years.

Key change, to another chorus of "Everybody Has Their Jubilee":

Everybody has their jubilee
Though sometimes the real things in life
Are difficult to see
Sometimes you're up, sometimes you're down
But it's all worth the fee
As long as
Everybody has their jubilee.

MARG:
I met a young lady
She was crying in her beer
A tragedy: I'll never be
A movie star, I fear
My nose and eyes I despise
'Cause I'm not on TV
I said, girl
You just might have missed your jubilee.

Everybody has their jubilee
Though sometimes the real things in life
Are difficult to see
Sometimes you're up, sometimes you're down
But it's all worth the fee
As long as
Everybody has their jubilee.

Instrumental break: a breakdown on fiddle. CHARLIE takes off his guitar and does a joyous step-dance, which he invites MARG to join. She politely declines, but then relents and dances a few steps, to general approval.

So don't you cry, all things must die
Don't fret about the past
Human dreams and human schemes
Were never meant to last
Today turns into yesterday
And that's just history
I say
Be careful you don't miss your jubilee.

Everybody has their jubilee
Though sometimes the real things in life
Are difficult to see
Sometimes you're up, sometimes you're down
But it's all worth the fee
As long as
Everybody has their jubilee.

After a key modulation and repeat chorus, the song ends, and the Islanders immediately break into the opening chords of "Smile the While," as the dancers waltz and RAE steps up gracefully to the microphone.

RAE: Well, that's our show, folks, and on behalf of Don, Marg, Charlie and the Islanders we want to thank you for coming out and for sticking with us as long as you did. We hope you think of us once in a while and maybe give a thought or two to yourselves while you're at it. And now just to say so long, here's Marg and Charlie to sing "Smile The While."

MARG and CHARLIE emerge from the dancers and sing "Smile the While":

Smile the while
You kiss me sad adieu
When the clouds roll by
I'll come to you
Then the sky will seem more blue
Down in Lovers' Lane, my dearie
Wedding bells will ring so merrily
Every tear will be a memory
So wait and pray each night for me
'Til we meet again.

The Islanders play a chorus as MARG and CHARLIE waltz, then sing:

Wedding bells will ring so merrily
Every tear will be a memory
So wait and pray each night for me
'Til we meet again
'Til we meet again.

The song ends. CHARLIE turns to MARG and kisses her hand. MARG smiles.

Curtain.